Performance Estimation of Computer Communication Networks
A Structured Approach

ELECTRICAL ENGINEERING, COMMUNICATIONS, AND SIGNAL PROCESSING

Raymond L. Pickholtz, Series Editor

IEEE Communication Society's Tutorials in Modern Communications
Victor B. Lawrence, Joseph L. Lo Cicero, and Laurence B. Milstein, Editors
Computer Network Architectures
Anton Meijer and Paul Peeters
Digital Transmission Systems and Networks, Volume I: Principles
Michael J. Miller and Syed V. Ahamed
Digital Transmission Systems and Networks, Volume II: Applications
Michael J. Miller and Syed V. Ahamed
Spread Spectrum Signal Design: LPE and AJ Systems
David L. Nicholson
Transmission Analysis in Communication Systems, Volume I
Osamu Shimbo
Spread Spectrum Communications, Volume I
Marvin K. Simon, Jim K. Omura, Robert A. Scholtz, and Barry K. Levitt
Spread Spectrum Communications, Volume II
Marvin K. Simon, Jim K. Omura, Robert A. Scholtz, and Barry K. Levitt
Spread Spectrum Communications, Volume III
Marvin K. Simon, Jim K. Omura, Robert A. Scholtz, and Barry K. Levitt
Performance Estimation of Computer Communication Networks: A Structured Approach
Pramode K. Verma
Elements of Digital Satellite Communication, Volume I: System Alternatives, Analyses, and Optimization
William W. Wu
Elements of Digital Satellite Communication, Volume II: Channel Coding and Integrated Services Digital Satellite Networks
William W. Wu
Current Advances in Distributed Computing and Communications
Yechiam Yemini

OTHER WORKS OF INTEREST

Local Area and Multiple Access Networks
Raymond L. Pickholtz, Editor
Telecommunications and the Law: An Anthology
Walter Sapronov, Editor

Performance Estimation of Computer Communication Networks
A Structured Approach

Pramode K. Verma
AT&T Bell Laboratories

COMPUTER SCIENCE PRESS

Dedicated to
the memory of
my parents

Library of Congress Cataloging-in-Publication Data

Verma, Pramode K.
  Performance estimation of computer communication networks: a structured approach.
    Includes index.
    1. Computer networks—Evaluation. 2. Computer networks—Reliability. I. Title.
TK5105.5.V47 1989   004.6   88-34221
ISBN 0-7167-8183-2

Copyright © 1989 Computer Science Press

No part of this book may be reproduced by any mechanical, photographic, or electronic process, or in the form of a phonographic recording, nor may it be stored in a retrieval system, transmitted, or otherwise copied for public or private use, without written permission from the publisher.

Printed in the United States of America

Computer Science Press
1803 Research Boulevard
Rockville, MD 20850

An imprint of W. H. Freeman and Company
41 Madison Avenue, New York, NY 10010
20 Beaumont Street, Oxford OX1 2NQ, England

1 2 3 4 5 6 7 8 9 0   RRD   7 6 5 4 3 2 1 0 8 9

CONTENTS

Preface ix

CHAPTER 1 EVOLUTION OF COMPUTER COMMUNICATION
NETWORK 1
1.1   TRANSITION TO AN INFORMATION SOCIETY 1
1.2   INFORMATION AND COMMUNICATION 2
1.3   COMPUTER COMMUNICATION NETWORKS 3
      1.3.1   Elements 3
      1.3.2   Resources 4
      1.3.3   Architecture 4
1.4   A HISTORY OF DEVELOPMENTS IN COMPUTER
      COMMUNICATION 5
1.5   REFERENCES 9

CHAPTER 2 CHARACTERIZATION OF A COMPUTER
COMMUNICATION NETWORK 11
2.1   A COMPUTER COMMUNICATION NETWORK
      MODEL 11
2.2   PERFORMANCE PARAMETERS 13
      2.2.1   Categories of Performance Parameters 13
      2.2.2   Delay Parameters 13
      2.2.3   Throughput Parameters 13
      2.2.4   Accuracy Parameters 14
      2.2.5   Availability Parameters 14
2.3   MAJOR ELEMENTS THAT DETERMINE
      PERFORMANCE 14
2.4   ASSESSMENT OF END-TO-END PERFORMANCE 14
2.5   PRICE 15
      2.5.1   Pricing Structure 15
      2.5.2   Start-up Cost 16
      2.5.3   Fixed Recurring Cost 16
      2.5.4   Usage-Sensitive Costs 16
      2.5.5   Addition, Reduction, and Rearrangement Costs 16
      2.5.6   Exit Costs 16

| | 2.5.7 | Displaced Costs | 17 |

CHAPTER 3 CHARACTERIZATION OF THE TRANSMISSION MEDIUM ... 18
3.1 THE TRANSMISSION MEDIUM ... 18
- 3.1.1 Capacity ... 18
- 3.1.2 Noise ... 20
- 3.1.3 Nyquist's Principle ... 20
- 3.1.4 Penalty of Noise ... 21
- 3.1.5 Limits of Signaling Speed and Bandwidth ... 22
- 3.1.6 Duobinary or Partial Response Coding Schemes ... 23
- 3.1.7 Extensions of Duobinary Transmission Schemes ... 25

3.2 TRANSMISSION MEDIUM FOR DIGITAL SIGNALS ... 27
- 3.2.1 Characteristics ... 27
- 3.2.2 Delay ... 29
- 3.2.3 Throughput ... 29
- 3.2.4 Integrity or Accuracy ... 32
- 3.2.5 Availability ... 33

3.3 REFERENCES ... 37

CHAPTER 4 NETWORK STATES AND HIERARCHIES OF PERFORMANCE ... 39
4.1 THE OPERATIONAL AND NONOPERATIONAL STATES OF A SYSTEM ... 39
4.2 NETWORK BEHAVIOR DURING AN OPERATIONAL STATE ... 40
4.3 COMPUTER COMMUNICATION NETWORKS ... 41
- 4.3.1 A Hierarchical View ... 41
- 4.3.2 The ISO/CCITT Layered Model ... 41
- 4.3.3 A Hierarchical Performance Model ... 42

4.4 REFERENCE ... 42

CHAPTER 5 TRANSMISSION-LEVEL PERFORMANCE ... 43
5.1 CHARACTERIZATION OF TRANSMISSION ACCURACY ... 43
5.2 BIT ERROR RATE ... 44
5.3 BLOCK TRANSMISSION ... 45
- 5.3.1 Block Error Rate ... 45
- 5.3.2 An Example ... 45

5.4 ERROR-FREE INTERVAL ... 46
- 5.4.1 Mean Error-Free Interval ... 46
- 5.4.2 MEFI knowing i Blocks in Error ... 47

5.5	ERROR-FREE SECONDS	54
5.6	SELECTING A TRANSMISSION MEDIUM	55
	5.6.1 Case Study 1	56
	5.6.2 Case Study 2	57
5.7	REFERENCES	58

CHAPTER 6 COMMUNICATION-LEVEL PERFORMANCE 59

6.1	SENSITIVITIES OF APPLICATIONS TO THE ERROR ENVIRONMENT	59
6.2	TECHNIQUES FOR ERROR CORRECTION	60
6.3	FORWARD ERROR CORRECTION	60
6.4	BACKWARD ERROR CORRECTION	62
6.5	IMPLICATIONS OF CYCLIC CODING	62
6.6	THE EFFECT OF PROPAGATION DELAY	66
6.7	CYCLIC REDUNDANCY CODING (CRC)	67
6.8	DEGREE OF PROTECTION FROM ERROR PROVIDED BY THE CYCLIC REDUNDANCY CODE	71
6.9	DELAY, THROUGHPUT, AND THE ERROR ENVIRONMENT	73
6.10	REFERENCES	73

CHAPTER 7 CUSTOMER PERCEIVED DELAYS IN A PACKET SWITCHED NETWORK 74

7.1	END-TO-END DELAYS	74
	7.1.1 Importance of End-to-End Delays	74
	7.1.2 End-to-End Delays in Packet Switched Networks	75
7.2	THE CHARACTER-AT-A-TIME TERMINAL	78
	7.2.1 Elements of End-to-End Delays	78
	7.2.2 Evaluation of Delay Components	80
	7.2.3 Summary of Results	82
7.3	THE BLOCK ORIENTED TERMINAL	82
	7.3.1 Elements of End-To-End Delays	82
	7.3.2 Summary of Results	84
7.4	NUMERICAL RESULTS	86
7.5	MESSAGE ASSEMBLY PROTOCOLS AND END-TO-END DELAYS	87
	7.5.1 The Influence of Message Assembly Protocols on End-to-End Delays	87
	7.5.2 The Model	87
	7.5.3 Analysis	88
	7.5.4 Numerical Results	92
7.6	PERCENTILE RESPONSE TIMES	95
7.7	THE PROPOSED METHOD	97

7.8	A CASE STUDY	99
7.9	APPENDIX 7A	103
	7.9.1 Statistics of the Last Packet of a Geometrically Distributed Message	103
7.10	APPENDIX 7B	104
	7.10.1 Statistics of the First Packet of a Geometrically Distributed Message	104
7.11	REFERENCES	105

CHAPTER 8   PERFORMANCE OBJECTIVES 107

8.1	NEED FOR PERFORMANCE OBJECTIVES	107
8.2	MAJOR DETERMINANTS OF PERFORMANCE OBJECTIVES	108
8.3	RELATIONSHIP BETWEEN PERFORMANCE PARAMETERS	108
8.4	OPTIMUM VALUE OF A PERFORMANCE PARAMETER	110
8.5	A NUMERICAL EXAMPLE	112

APPENDIX   NETWORK SWITCHING TECHNIQUES AND THEIR CHARACTERISTICS 116

A.1	AN OVERVIEW OF A NETWORK	116
A.2	TYPES OF SWITCHING	116
A.3	MESSAGE SWITCHING	122
A.4	PACKET SWITCHING	122
	A.4.1 Further Characteristics of Packet Switching	124
A.5	CHARACTER SWITCHING	127
A.6	REFERENCES	130

INDEX 131

ABOUT THE AUTHOR 133

PREFACE

This book is aimed at the practicing professional in computer communication. It addresses issues related to the end-to-end performance estimation of computer communication systems, especially in the context of a common-user network environment. Private computer communication networks addressing either a variety of applications for a single customer (owner) or serving a number of customers but addressing a single application can be considered to be special cases of a common-user network. The absence of a suitable book with particular emphasis on end-to-end performance has been felt by many practicing professionals engaged in the development, design, evaluation, or use of computer communication networks and systems. A potential network customer is particularly handicapped if a reliable means to estimate end-to-end performance is unavailable prior to a long-term and potentially heavy financial or operational commitment. This book can also be used as the main text for a one-semester graduate course in computer communication networks if supplemented by other current references depending upon the need and background of the student body.

Computer communication is a rapidly changing technology. The emphasis in this book is therefore on so structuring the overall problem of performance estimation that the implications of the various factors affecting performance are clearly understood. Examples are used to acquaint the reader with realistic ranges of performance parameters.

Chapter 1 presents a history of developments in computer communication systems. It analyzes these developments in light of available technologies and the magnitude and diversity of overall demand and users' expectations of system performance. The currently adopted networking approach in computer communication is shown to result from maturing technologies, higher overall demands, and customers' needs for flexibility, ubiquity, and higher performance.

Chapter 2 characterizes a computer communication network in terms of functionality and performance. Each of these aspects is described in terms of a set of parameters. A conceptual model that can be used to select alternative networks is presented. Chapter 3 presents a characterization of the transmission medium and the transmission process from a performance standpoint.

Chapter 4 addresses the two states of a network — operational and non-operational — from a user's standpoint. It also introduces the concepts of transmission-level performance and communication-level performance. It explains the hierarchical relationship between the two sets of parameters quantifying performance at these two levels and shows how the end-to-end performance can be assessed in terms of these sets of parameters. Chapter 5 characterizes the transmission-level parameters and points out how they can be estimated. Chapter 6 introduces the concept of error correction in the transmission process and examines the trade-off between a better error environment and additional delay or lower throughput. Chapter 7 furnishes a methodology to estimate user perceived performance in a packet switched network. Chapter 8 discusses performance objectives and proposes a method by which performance objectives can be set to reflect the need of the user in a resource-limited environment.

The Appendix presents a comparative evaluation of switching techniques, especially packet and circuit switching. The applicability of each switching technique for a particular traffic and application class is emphasized. The Appendix may be used as a review resource by the reader.

In concluding these opening remarks, I would like to express my gratitude to my colleagues at Bell Laboratories, several of whom read through the manuscript and provided valuable suggestions. I am also indebted to AT&T for permission to publish the work. Finally, I would like to pay tribute to my wife, Gita, and to my daughter, Pallavi, who patiently endured my absence during the writing process.

Pramode K. Verma

Chapter 1

EVOLUTION OF COMPUTER COMMUNICATION NETWORKS*

This chapter presents a history of developments in computer communication systems. It points out the gradual evolution of modern society into an information society and the importance of the movement and management of data in an information society. It further analyzes developments in data communication in light of the needs of the user and the available technology.

1.1 TRANSITION TO AN INFORMATION SOCIETY

Modern society is rapidly evolving into an information society. Our ability to transform, communicate, and store information has produced some fundamental changes in the manner in which businesses are conducted, government operations are run, educational institutions function, and so forth, compared to what existed just a few decades ago. Even more revolutionary changes are yet to come and are expected to arrive at an increasingly faster rate. But just what is information and why is it so important, and why is it going to be more important or pervasive in the future?

From an abstract point of view, availability of information is tantamount to removal of uncertainty. The higher the degree of uncertainty removed, the larger the amount of information provided. But is information an abstract object or a tangible commodity?

---

* Portions of this chapter are reprinted, with permission, from *So This Is 1984*, D. Parkhill and P. Enslow, Jr., Eds., © Elsevier Science Publishers B.V., 1984, essay entitled "A 1984 Perspective on Developments in Computer Communication," by P. K. Verma, pp. 43-48.

In today's world, information functions as a tangible commodity but with some specific characteristics inapplicable to most other commodities [1]. Like any other commodity, it can be sold or exchanged; it can also substitute for human labor, materials, or energy. The great savings of human labor realized through information transforming (or more commonly, information processing) machines are well known. Further, better information handling techniques can directly result in material savings; for example, better signaling techniques can enhance the utilization of railroad tracks. Similarly, modern teleconferencing techniques, which allow geographically separated individuals to interact, provide a substitute for face-to-face meetings, and thus result in considerable savings of energy. Unlike materials or energy, however, information can be duplicated or multiplied indefinitely at very little additional cost. Further, it can be readily and compactly stored, and it is well known that the costs of storing information are rapidly decreasing.

1.2 INFORMATION AND COMMUNICATION

Information may exist in more than one format. Data, speech, or image signals present information. Information may be handled, that is, processed, stored, or transmitted, using different techniques depending upon its origin and the format in which it exists. The handling techniques employed in a specific situation are also governed by the performance requirements of the specific application or usage under consideration and cost objectives. In general, improvement of performance requires additional costs being incurred.

When communication takes place between two end points or entities — human beings, terminals, or programs in execution, information is the commodity that is transported or exchanged. We define communication between two entities as a programmed response(s) to a stimulus or stimuli originating from one or more entities and conveyed to appropriate destinations. Communication thus includes processing and storage. Communication is not necessarily just a bilateral association, it could in general be many to many. Further, the vector of stimuli has not merely combinational but also sequential significance.

I define data as any machine-originated information in digital format. Note that both the source or origin and the format of the information are specified in this definition. Speech may exist in a digital format and may be transmitted as such using the techniques of pulse code modulation. However, it does not qualify as data. The reason for making this distinction arises from purely practical considerations. For example, in a transmission system designed for digitized voice, the two communicating ends may lose synchronization and therefore virtually lose communication (for say, 40 milliseconds) without noticeably degraded performance on the user's part. Such a loss of synchronization would, however, be unacceptable for the data user for most applications, unless the system designer insures that the effect of such a temporary loss of communication is not visible at the user or application level. Performance requirements thus govern system design and are in turn derived from the end user's perception of the service.

Data has been defined as machine-originated information in digital format. The signals which two digital machines use to communicate with each other are data. The necessity for machines to communicate with each other can be viewed as a necessary step in the evolution of modern society. Man invented machines to lighten his tasks. For more sophisticated machines, it was necessary to communicate in a more formal and sophisticated manner and man-machine interfaces of varying degrees of complexity were set up. The next step in this evolutionary process was to develop interfaces directly between machines, without the necessity of any human involvement. The communication between one digital machine and another over a distance is one example of two machines interacting directly. We can thus consider computer communication as the scientific discipline which deals with the remote interaction and cooperation among digital machines.

As stated earlier, we are rapidly moving toward an information society. Growing dependence on information has become a part of everyday life. Data is the most rapidly growing part of the entire realm of the information world. One reason behind this phenomenon is the rapidly increasing need for information or computer power to be accessible from and available at a remote point. In general, one may say that the greatest value of information is realized not when it is static but when it moves and is shared.

1.3 COMPUTER COMMUNICATION NETWORKS

1.3.1 Elements

A computer communication network is a collection of nodes and interconnecting transmission channels. Nodes are responsible for signal processing, and include sources and sinks of information. Transmission channels convey information from one node to another and are characterized by channel capacity, a finite (but usually constant) delay and a distribution function for errors. An element of distance between nodes is implicit in the definition of a network; in fact this is what distinguishes a *network* from a *system*. As a general rule, a transmission line employed *within a system* to interconnect two devices is considered to be a tight coupling device. Should the performance of the transmission line be comparable to that of the devices it interconnects, or start influencing the overall performance to a significant degree, it can no longer be considered to be a tight coupling device. Under these conditions, the system, however small physically, starts behaving like a network. In summary, then, the nodes of a computer communication network are somewhat loosely interconnected through imperfect transmission channels of specified (and constant) capacity, (usually constant) delay, and a distribution function for errors. The overall behavior of a network is strongly influenced by the interconnecting transmission channels, usually in a statistically predictable way. The main advantage of networks arises from the sharing of resources they provide. No network needs to be able to meet peak demands imposed from all of its subscribers at the same time. This requires every network to have a discipline to allocate its resources to demands and a mechanism to resolve contention should it occur. Computer communication networks are also referred to as information networks.

1.3.2 Resources

The resources of an information network are physically distributed and could be broadly characterized under (i) processing, (ii) storage, and (iii) transport. Processing involves manipulating the bits with or without changing the semantic content of the original bit stream(s). Storage provides explicit control over information insofar as introducing deliberate delay at any point during its residence within the network is concerned. Transport is the function associated with transferring a bit from one point to another.

1.3.3 Architecture

Even though physically distributed, the resources of a computer communication network can work cooperatively in accomplishing a single function. For example, consider a network where the processing resources are physically distributed. If the peak hours associated with the different processing nodes are different, the peak-hour processing capacity of a particular node can be augmented by the spare capacity available at a different node which has a different peak hour associated with it. This flexibility gives a network solution an advantage in terms of handling the overall demand relative to non-network solutions where a fixed assignment of resources to tasks exists.

Network architecture deals with the overall framework under which resources of the network are organized and managed in order to meet the demands imposed on it. One may think of network architectures in which one or more of its resources are either highly centralized or fully distributed, or where the processing resources are either all functionally identical or segregated in groups to perform specific tasks.

Network architecture is driven not only by the anticipated demand to which the network will be subjected, but also by the trade-off between its fundamental resources — processing, storage, and transport. Further, for any network, particularly for a common user network, user demand profiles evolve and change over time. Similarly, the network's primary constituents (i.e., resources) evolve in terms of their price-performance characteristics. These two sets of variables make it necessary that the network architect not only understand customers' current usage patterns and the price-performance characteristics of the network building blocks, but also anticipate how these variables are likely to evolve over a period of time equal to the anticipated design life of the network.

A procedure to synthesize a computer communication network architecture is well beyond our present reach. In practice, one starts with one or more hypothetical architectures. These architectures are then realized using available components and systems. The best of these, using some criteria, then becomes the chosen architecture. Flexibility in meeting unpredictable future need is one key criterion.

1.4 A HISTORY OF DEVELOPMENTS IN COMPUTER COMMUNICATION

When the need for data to be transported over a distance first arose, the telephone network could expeditiously and economically meet that need (see Figure 1.1). Existing network procedures and protocols were used to set up calls. Once an end-to-end physical channel was set up, the use of a modem allowed digital signals to be transported over an analog medium (see Section 3.1).

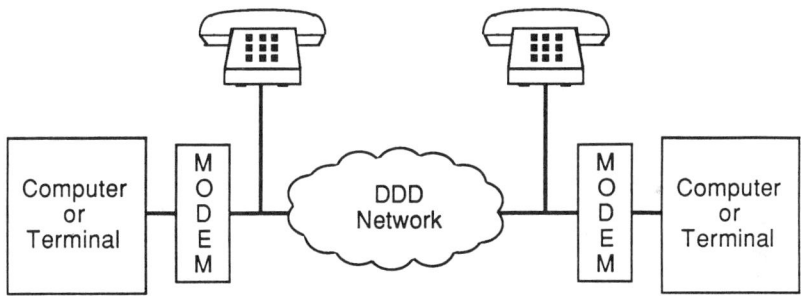

Characteristics
- Ubiquitous
- One circuit (3 kHz) per connection
- Performance governed by the voice network
- Lack of flexibility

Figure 1.1
The Initial Approach

The telephone network could be characterized by three attributes: (i) ubiquity, (ii) a fixed bandwidth of 4 kHz nominal or 3.1 kHz actual, and (iii) a level of performance designed primarily to meet the needs of voice communication. Ubiquity was a favorable factor in the use of the voice network since it provided an almost universal accessibility. The fixed bandwidth of the telephone network was a definite disadvantage, since it was uneconomic to use the entire bandwidth if the machine speed was low. For example, an asynchronous (start-stop) machine operating at a line speed of 110 baud will experience a nominal information transmission efficiency of 80/4000 or 0.02 bits/sec/Hz, assuming 11 bits are transmitted on line per 8-bit character. The fixed bandwidth was also a disadvantage if the user needed a speed of transmission higher than what the 3.1 kHz bandwidth could accommodate.

The telecommunication carriers' reaction in the early seventies to meeting the performance and flexibility requirements of the data communication user, in an economic way, was the provisioning of data transmission networks. A data transmission network is a collection of nodes interconnected by transmission facilities which provides point-to-point communication only (i.e., the source-sink relationship between network end points is invariant with time). These networks are also referred to as private line networks or as networks providing private line service. The first such commercial network was the TransCanada Telephone System's Dataroute [2]. This was followed by AT&T's Digital Data System [3]. Both these networks resulted in enhanced performance and greater economy and flexibility to the user.

The two digital data transmission networks mentioned above are nothing but networks of transmission facilities. First established for the transportation of voice in analog format, these transmission facilities were digitized for efficient data transmission. The costs associated with the advance digitalization of the existing telephone plant for data transmission was easily paid for by the users' benefiting from lower cost per bit and higher performance. In retrospect, it is important to note that the needs of the data user added to the momentum to digitize the telephone network, intended initially for speech communication.

In the two data transmission networks referred to above, the transmission resources for voice and data are derived from the same physical facility (e.g., the same microwave system). However, the same transmission channel could not carry voice and data interchangeably. This is referred to as functional separation. In the functionally separate (analog) voice and (digital) data transmission environments, it was possible to regenerate data signals as frequently as desired. Selective regeneration of data signals was impossible in an integrated transmission environment where facilities could be used interchangeably to transport voice in the analog format and data in the digital format. The ability to regenerate data signals was the key element in improving transmission performance.

A transmission network alone is not sufficient for effective data communication. Provisioning of transmission is just one step in meeting the total communication needs. To meet total communication needs by a transmission network alone would require physical transmission channels between each and every end point. For n end points, it would mean $n(n-1)/2$ transmission channels would be needed to provide a full interconnection between all end points. This is clearly an undesirable solution for a large number of end points, or when all end points have no need in general to be simultaneously communicating with each other.

The teleprocessing applications, which have existed since the fifties, first used the telephone network, as discussed earlier, for meeting all their data transmission needs. During the 1960s, the teleprocessing requirements gave rise to the arrangement shown in Figure 1.2. It was a private network approach composed of leased lines and remote or local concentrators using a star topology.

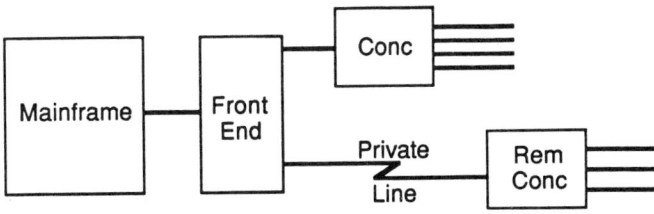

Characteristics

- Communications sub-net replaced the physical lines through TDM or ATDM network

- Computer knows the exact type of terminal that will appear at a given point

Figure 1.2
The Next Approach

A typical example of this arrangement is the IBM System/360 running BTAM. Essentially, all the processing was concentrated in the central host processor, befitting the technology available at the time. The front end was a transmission control unit responsible for only elementary Data Link Control (DLC) functions. There was lack of line sharing or terminal sharing. A given line and all terminals on it were part of the access path to only one application program. Access to two different applications required two terminals and two lines [4].

The above handicap was corrected with the release around 1974 of System/370 with software and hardware releases referred to as SNA. The front end became a programmable communication controller doing DLC and a great deal more. The design allowed terminals to share a line to separate applications located in the same host.

However, from an overall systems point of view, the private network approach also resulted in a fragmented approach to solving the needs of data communications users. This approach was potentially expensive for the smaller customer due to lack of sufficient sharing. Lack of interconnectability among private networks was another factor of importance to many users.

The preceding considerations suggested the need for adopting a shared network approach, rather than a fragmented approach, to data communications. A network is not merely a collection of terminals, communication lines, and computers but is an organized structure to which computers and terminals attach and through which they communicate. Such a network should have the ability to connect all instruments that meet a defined set of access and protocol requirements. Ordinarily, in such a network any entity should be able to communicate to any other port or to any 'process' owned by a port. Public data networks are today in existence in several countries. Most such networks operate on the principle of packet switching. Considering the developments that have taken place during the last five years, one can conclude that the network approach to computer communications has become an established way of providing communication between computers and terminals. The shared network approach to data communications is illustrated in Figure 1.3. From a general point of view, a network should be responsible for the collection, storage, processing, transmission, and distribution of information [5].

A high-level machine-to-machine communication between two end points demands much more than a simple transport connection. As an example of a higher-level communication, consider the following: When two human beings interact over a telephone, a good voice-band (4-kHz nominal) connection is a necessary requirement. However, before they can meaningfully converse with each other, they must speak the same language, and even within the same language where words have multiple meanings, they must have some means for resolving ambiguities should they arise. In addition, there usually are information interchange questions related to the confirmation of transmission. Redialing the number is a way to reestablish communication should the connection be broken. On a redialed connection, the communicating parties usually identify where they were cut off, in order to assure continuity.

Transport requirements are basic to all higher level communication functions. An efficient transport network is thus a necessary part of computer communication. The transport network can be viewed as a basic structure over which higher level communication functions are built.

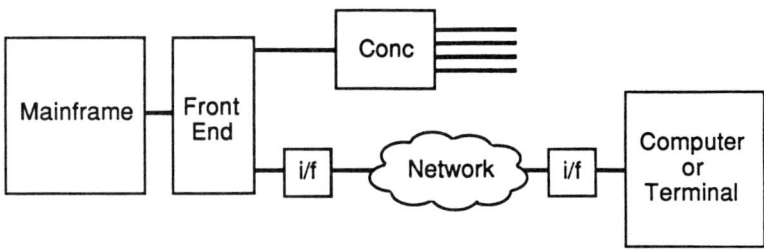

Characteristics

- Same terminal capable of communicating to a variety of terminals/computers

- Network requires standard communication protocols

Figure 1.3
The Network Approach

In this book we adopt a structured approach in developing performance assessment techniques for computer communication networks. Our primary emphasis is on the transport function associated with a computer communication network. The perspective adopted is that of a user.

1.5 REFERENCES

[1] Colin Cherry, *On Human Communications,* Third Edition, 1978. The MIT Press, Chapter I.

[2] D. J. Horton and P. G. Bowie, "An Overview of Dataroute: System and Performance," in Proc., Int. Conf. Comm., Minneapolis, June, 1974, pp. 2A1-2A5.

[3] N. E. Snow and N. Knapp, Jr., "Digital Data System — System Overview," The Bell System Technical Journal, Vol. 54, No. 5, May-June 1975, pp. 811-832.

[4] P. E. Green, Jr., "An Introduction to Network Architectures and Protocols," IEEE Trans. on Comm., Vol. Com-28, No. 12, April 1980, pp. 412-424.

[5] D. Parkhill and P. Enslow, Jr., eds., "A 1984 Perspective on Developments in Computer Communication Systems," *So This Is 1984*, Elsevier Science Publishers B. V., 1984, pp. 43-48.

Chapter 2

CHARACTERIZATION OF A COMPUTER COMMUNICATION NETWORK

This chapter characterizes a computer communication network in terms of its functionality, performance, and price. These are the three dimensions in which users' views of a network can be presented. The chapter further discusses the parameters of performance and the factors that influence the end-to-end performance perceived by the user.

2.1 A COMPUTER COMMUNICATION NETWORK MODEL

Figure 2.1 shows an example of a Computer Communication Network across which two entities are communicating. Entity 1 might be a terminal connected to the network using an access subsystem; similarly, entity 2 might be a host connected to the network using another access subsystem. The network is the medium over which communication takes place.

The user may be viewed as accomplishing a task, such as a file update at, or retrieval of information from, the host. From the user's perspective, the entire operation can be viewed in the following three dimensions:

- Functionality
- Performance
- Price

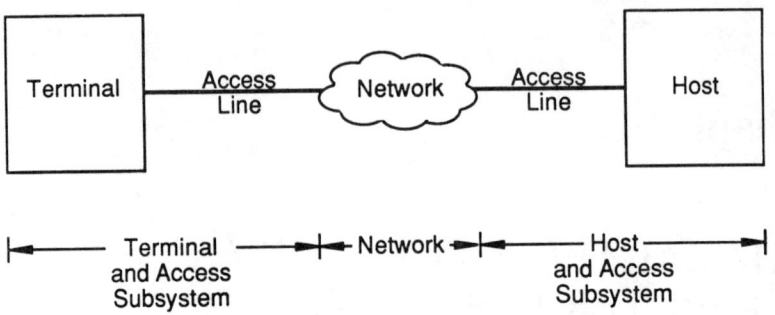

Figure 2.1
Major Components of a Computer Communication Network

Functionality is the totality of functions that the user is concerned with in the application. A relatively complex application such as an order processing application might be composed of a number of less complex functions, such as information search and retrieval, file update, and so on. Functionality is directly related to the task at hand. If the network, in conjunction with the user's equipment, is not capable of providing all the functions that are needed in serving an application, then it is of no value to a potential user of that application. For example, if a network provides no storage capability, then an application requiring information delivery from the network at an instant of time specified by the user cannot be served using resources of the network.

Functionality is not absolute, however. It must be further qualified by a set of performance parameters (the second dimension) which are meaningful to the application under consideration, and whose values are of consequence in judging the degree of effectiveness with which the application requirements are being met. The third dimension — price — is the total cost to the user that could be attributed to the application under consideration.

Our emphasis in this book is on performance, especially communications performance. In comparing available solutions, each of which meets the requirements of a given task, one enumerates the list of meaningful performance parameters which characterize that task. Performance values or levels are then tabulated in terms of each of the listed parameters for all alternatives.

If the performance levels needed for the task are known, then those alternatives that are deficient in terms of one or more parameters can be eliminated, making a shorter list of acceptable alternatives. One technique frequently used in computer communication systems design is to choose the least-cost alternative from among the acceptable ones.

Performance levels specified in terms of the chosen parameters will generally differ for each acceptable alternative. Unfortunately, however, since the set of performance parameters cannot be transformed into a single scalar quantity, a single figure of merit from a performance perspective cannot in general be derived. It may, however, be possible to derive one under certain specific situations. Lack of a single performance parameter makes the task of comparing several solutions on the basis of performance very challenging indeed. Strategic factors often play a leading role in determining the solution adopted.

2.2 PERFORMANCE PARAMETERS

2.2.1 Categories of Performance Parameters

Four categories of performance parameters are useful from the user's perspective. These are:

- Delay related performance parameters, or delay parameters
- Throughput related performance parameters, or throughput parameters
- Integrity related performance parameters, or accuracy parameters
- Availability related performance parameters, or availability parameters

2.2.2 Delay Parameters

Delay parameters are a class of parameters affecting the user's ability to control the duration of time within which a desired outcome or an event takes place. For example, in the case of an information retrieval application, the time within which the desired response is received, after being requested, is a parameter of considerable importance to the user. We shall see later that parameters such as these are themselves functions of several other parameters characterizing a network.

2.2.3 Throughput Parameters

Throughput parameters quantify the total volume of work the user can accomplish in a given amount of time. For example, in applications where a large file is to be transmitted, the effective rate at which the channel is transmitting information, or the channel throughput, is an important parameter. The absolute delay between the transmission and the reception of information, within bounds, is relatively unimportant.

It may appear at first that delay and throughput are inversely related. This is not the case. For example, a satellite channel has a large delay associated with it, but it can provide a very high throughput for one-way information transfer with the use of an appropriate protocol.

2.2.4 Accuracy Parameters

Accuracy related parameters quantify the integrity of transmission, that is, the accuracy of the message as well as the accuracy of the delivery process. Every message or packet that flows across a network contains a destination address. Both the message and the address are subject to transmission errors. A bit error in the address space will result in misdelivery. Occasionally, both the address and the message may contain errors.

2.2.5 Availability Parameters

A communication system is termed unavailable when it is not able to function as designed or when its performance has degraded below a predetermined threshold so that effective communication cannot take place. Recovery from unavailability may be automatic, such as after a period of resynchronization, or manual, as, for example, when a working part has failed and needs to be replaced manually. The user needs to understand the statistical characteristics of unavailability in order to be able to design the end-to-end system effectively.

2.3 MAJOR ELEMENTS THAT DETERMINE PERFORMANCE

The end-to-end performance of the arrangement shown in Figure 2.1 can be compartmentalized into three major components: the access subsystem at the terminal end, the network, and the access subsystem at the host computer end. Each of these three major components can be characterized by a number of performance parameters in each of the four performance categories referred to above. Note that the access subsystem includes the corresponding end point as well.

Either of the access subsystems shown could be one of a variety of options such as: dial-up (or circuit switched) connection, private line circuit, or private line multipoint circuit. After the initial delay in setting up a circuit, the dial-up circuit behaves like a private line circuit. A multipoint circuit is a single private line circuit with several terminals sharing it. (See Figure 2.2). Sharing a single line among a number of terminals allows economies in the access resource. The multipoint line and the terminals it supports must use a discipline in order to ensure an orderly sharing of the transmission line among the terminals. Polling is one such means.

2.4 ASSESSMENT OF END-TO-END PERFORMANCE

As discussed in Section 2.3, the access subsystems and the network together determine the user perceived performance. For a given set of user requirements, considerable variations in performance can be obtained by choosing different access subsystems.

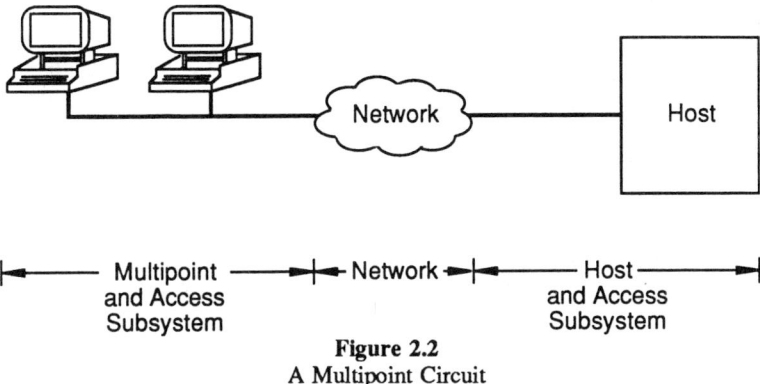

Figure 2.2
A Multipoint Circuit

Potentially, the access subsystems and the network may be owned by two or more different organizational entities. This requires the user to do business with two or more different organizations in realizing a single business application. Understanding the performance parameters of the different components that constitute an end-to-end system is even more important in a multi-supplier environment, since in this case no single supplier could guarantee the end-to-end performance.

The end-to-end or user perceived performance can be assessed in terms of characteristics of the following elements:

- User's traffic
- Access subsystems including terminals and/or host computers
- The network

User's traffic is, in general, characterized in terms of its statistical properties, such as, distribution of message lengths, their arrival/generation characteristics, and so on. Each of the access subsystems is characterized in terms of applicable parameters representing the four categories of performance parameters discussed in Section 2.2. The network is similarly characterized in terms of the applicable performance parameters.

2.5 PRICE

2.5.1 Pricing Structure

The price a user pays for meeting the needs of his or her application is obviously an important, and often the decisive, factor in his or her choice of the specific arrangement. In a competitive environment, price or price packaging is often used by different vendors to differentiate among their product or service offerings. For this reason, implications of the pricing structure for a common-user-network service offering may not always be easy to understand. In the following subsections, we present the elements of the pricing structure that need to be explicitly considered in determining the overall implications of cost to the user incurred in connection with meeting the total needs of an application.

2.5.2 Start-up Cost

This is a one-time fee associated with signing up for a common user network service.

2.5.3 Fixed Recurring Cost

This is a fixed periodic (e.g., monthly) charge to maintain subscription to the service. The charge is independent of any usage and could be subject to change depending upon market conditions.

2.5.4 Usage-Sensitive Costs

Usage-sensitive costs are applicable to all situations where users draw upon a common pool of network resources. An example of a situation where it is not applicable is a private line service where, in effect, the entire resources of the point-to-point service are available to the customer whether or not these resources are used by the customer. For a common user, packet switched network, the usage-sensitive costs may depend upon the number of virtual circuits established and the number of packets transmitted.

2.5.5 Addition, Reduction, and Rearrangement Costs

Since the needs for all services vary with time, costs associated with changes in the arrangement subscribed to are important factors that should be considered by a customer. It is usually easy to overlook this factor because changes and rearrangements are hard to predict. However, costs related to addition, reduction, and rearrangement must be considered if two alternatives are going to be compared properly.

2.5.6 Exit Costs

Many service offerings require subscriptions for minimum periods of time. Termination of the service by a customer may require him or her to pay the fixed recurring cost for the remaining term of the original contract. In addition, termination of a particular service and subscription to another service may have cost implications by way of additional user training, new terminal or interface equipment, and so on.

2.5.7 Displaced Costs

In considering a replacement for an existing service, the sum total of the cost associated with the new service and adjusted for the periodicity associated with the different elements of cost, must be balanced against the cost of the present system. The displaced cost includes the financial impact due to reduction in equipment as well as personnel.

I have examined in this chapter the three dimensions that characterize a computer communication network from a user's standpoint. My goal in this book is to address the performance dimension, specifically the user perceived performance, in terms of the characteristics of the elements that constitute the end-to-end system. Before we do that, however, we must be able to characterize each of the elements individually. This is taken up in the next chapter.

Chapter 3

CHARACTERIZATION OF THE TRANSMISSION MEDIUM

This chapter presents a characterization of the transmission medium and the transmission process. Characteristics of the transmission medium in terms of the performance parameters discussed earlier are described. Basic characteristics of synchronous and asynchronous transmission are explained.

3.1 THE TRANSMISSION MEDIUM

3.1.1 Capacity

A transmission medium is a basic element of a communication network. Physically, it may take the form of twisted pairs of copper wire, coaxial cable, optical fiber, open space, and so on. As discussed earlier, a transmission medium interconnects the nodes of a computer communication network.

Contrary to popular notions, a transmission medium is not intrinsically analog or digital. Any of the media referred to in the previous paragraph can be used for transmitting analog or digital signals. If digital signals are transmitted over the transmission medium, regenerative or digital repeaters are deployed at intervals commensurate with adequate performance. In the case of analog signals, amplifiers or repeaters are deployed throughout the length of a transmission medium to ensure an adequate signal-to-noise ratio at the destination. The fact whether a transmission medium is using analog amplifiers or digital repeaters can be used to determine whether it is being used to carry information in analog or digital format.

In Chapter 1, I defined data as machine-originated information in digital format. In other words, data is always digital. The same transmission medium can transmit analog and digital signals alternately. The switched telephone network used to transmit data, which is digital, provides an example in point.

The end-to-end telephone network, as exemplified by two telephones in communication, can be considered to be a band-pass filter in the frequency domain between the frequencies of 300 Hz and 3400 Hz approximately. Data, in its baseband format, cannot be transmitted over this channel. Use of a modem which converts digital signals into pulses of frequencies acceptable within the pass band of the transmission medium can allow data to be transmitted at bit rates, within acceptable bounds of error, that could be estimated. (See Figure 1.1.)

C. E. Shannon [1] in 1948 developed a relationship between channel bandwidth in hertz and transmission capacity in bits per second. The relationship can be expressed mathematically as

$$C = W \log_2(1 + S/N) \qquad (3.1)$$

where C is the channel capacity in bits per second, W is the bandwidth in Hertz, and S and N are the power levels associated with the signal and the noise, respectively.

Equation (3.1) gives an upper bound of channel capacity under ideal conditions. If we consider a telephone channel with the following bandwidth and signal-to-noise ratio characteristics:

$$W = 3000 \text{ Hz}$$

$$\frac{S}{N} = 30 \text{ dB or } 10^3$$

then;

$$C = 3000 \log_2(1 + 1000)$$

$$= 29{,}880 \text{ bits/sec.} \qquad (3.2)$$

As stated, Equation (3.2) represents an upper bound. This capacity cannot be attained in practice due to the following reasons: (i) the telephone transmission medium is not distortionless, and (ii) the noise power within the channel is not uniformly distributed. These two assumptions are necessary in deriving Equation (3.1). However, even if these assumptions held, attainment of a channel capacity given by Equation (3.2) might still be impracticable because the Shannon limit would require a very complex encoding scheme. In practice, a telephone channel's capacity is generally limited to 9600 bits/sec over a dialed channel, and 19,200 bits/sec over a conditioned private line. Modems working at 19,200 bits/sec have been developed and reported recently [2], but it is unlikely that the modem technology for use over a voice-band channel will advance much beyond this speed, for the reasons presented above.

3.1.2 Noise

A binary transmission system has two symbols usually designated as 1 and 0. Should each of these symbols be *equally likely to occur* an information of one bit is associated with the occurrence of each symbol. In general, an m-ary system with m symbols or levels of transmission, where the ith symbol occurs with the probability p_i, the average amount of information per symbol is given by [1]

$$I = -\sum_{i=1}^{m} p_i \log_2 p_i \quad \frac{\text{bits}}{\text{symbol}} \qquad (3.3)$$

It can be easily seen that the I given above is maximized when all the p_i's are equal, that is, when $p_i = 1/m$. Under this condition, the maximum amount of information associated with the occurrence of any symbol or alphabet is given by

$$I_{\max} = \log_2 m \quad \frac{\text{bits}}{\text{symbol}} \qquad (3.4)$$

3.1.3 Nyquist's Principle

Early in the telegraph transmission days, Nyquist got concerned with establishing the relationship between the rate at which signals could be transmitted in a band-limited medium. Nyquist's famous result states that the transmission of N signal elements per second requires a (theoretical) minimum bandwidth of $N/2$ Hz.

A signal element is not necessarily intended to convey one bit of information. It could carry several bits of information. If a signal element could assume m possible levels, all of which were equally likely, each element would represent $\log_2 m$ bits of information. The amount of information that could be carried in unit band-width of the transmission medium is therefore bounded by a theoretical maximum of $2 \log_2 m$ bits/sec. It should be noted that m cannot be indefinitely increased. Its maximum value is limited by the presence of noise and the difficulty associated with accurate detection as *m* is increased.

3.1.4 Penalty of Noise

It was mentioned in the earlier section that noise limits the maximum number of detectable levels which a signal element can have. An approximate computation can easily be made to quantify the magnitude of this penalty.

Assume that a binary system represents its two possible levels 0 and 1 by 0 volts and A volts respectively. A threshold is set at $A/2$ volts such that all received signals of magnitudes equal to or less than $A/2$ volts are interpreted as 0 while all signals with higher voltage levels are represented as 1. This is illustrated diagrammatically in Figure 3.1.

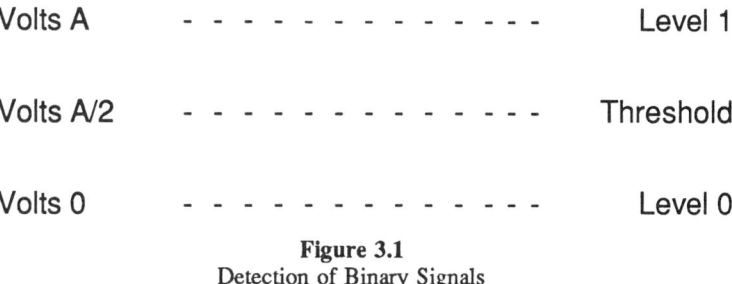

Figure 3.1
Detection of Binary Signals

The threshold for a binary system, as discussed above, is given by

$$D_b = A/2 \qquad (3.5)$$

Assume next that the 0 to A volt range consists of m levels. The threshold of voltage for distinguishing a level from its adjacent level is now reduced to

$$D_m = \frac{A}{2(m-1)} \qquad (3.6)$$

The level of noise permitted ordinarily for proper functioning of the system should be less than D_b or D_m for a binary or for an m-ary system, respectively.

The noise penalty for an m-ary system relative to a binary system can now be written as

$$\text{Noise penalty} = 20 \log_{10}(D_b/D_m)$$

$$= 20 \log_{10}(m-1) \text{ dB} \qquad (3.7)$$

3.1.5 Limits of Signaling Speed and Bandwidth

It was mentioned in Section 3.1.3 that the maximum signaling speed in a channel of bandwidth W is $2W$ signal elements per second. For binary transmission systems, the maximum channel capacity is therefore limited to $2W$ bits per second, since each element can carry a maximum of 1 bit of information.

The transmission efficiency of a transmission system is defined as the information transmission rate per unit of bandwidth. Using this definition, it could be concluded that the theoretical maximum transmission efficiency of a binary system is 2 bits/sec/Hz. This maximum signaling speed can be obtained only under ideal conditions. To understand this, consider pulses of the waveform shown in Figure 3.2.

Transmission Rates

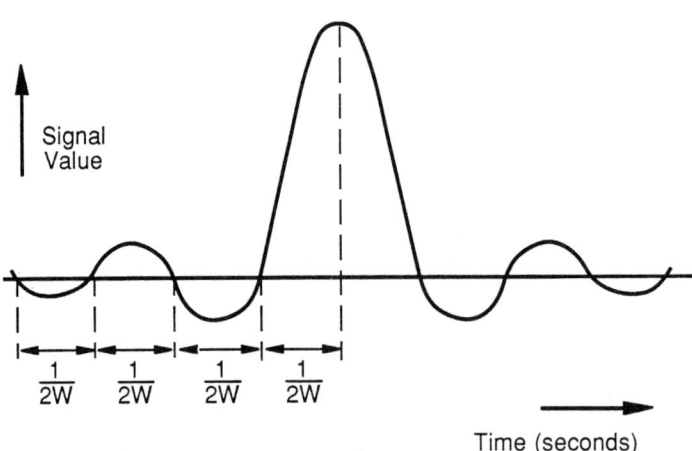

Figure 3.2
Pulse Waveform Transmitting Information at the Nyquist Rate

Such pulses have peaks separated by $1/2W$ seconds. The peaks of each pulse coincide with the zeros of other pulses, so there is no interference between the different pulses if sampling is made to coincide with pulse peaks. The energy-density spectrum (i.e., the distribution of energy over the different frequencies) of these pulses can be shown to be constant from 0 to W Hz and zero over all higher frequencies.

It can also be shown that a signal, band-limited to W Hz, cannot assume an infinite number of independent values per second. It can, in fact, assume only $2W$ independent values per second [1].

It follows, therefore, that the maximum transmission efficiency of a binary transmission system is 2 bits/sec/Hz. From a practical point of view, this maximum cannot be attained. In general, the minimum channel bandwidth must be greater than half the signaling rate for satisfactory performance. Multilevel coding can help reduce the bandwidth requirement. This is discussed in the next section.

3.1.6 Duobinary or Partial Response Coding Schemes [3]

A binary signal can be changed into an m-ary signal (or a multi-level signal) to reduce the number of signal elements per second that must be sent. For example, if binary signals are changed into quaternary signals, each signal element will represent two bits of information and the signaling speed requirement on the transmission channel can be halved. The price one has to pay for accomplishing this is a higher noise immunity requirement, as discussed in Section 3.1.3.

In a duobinary system, encoding and decoding of a signal involves dealing with the algebraic sum of the value of the present digit and of the previous digit. To accomplish this, a binary input is passed through a shaping filter having a transfer function which delays the waveform one interval and adds it to itself. As a result, the original two-level signal is transformed into a three-level signal formed by an algebraic addition of the present and the previous pulse.

Let $A_{k-n}, A_{k-n+1}, \ldots, A_{k-1}, A_k, A_{k+1} \ldots$ be the binary symbols occurring at instants of time $-n, -n+1, \ldots, 1, 0, 1, \ldots$.

At $t = 0$, the signal on line is $Y_k = A_k + A_{k-1}$.

The duobinary encoding scheme is shown in Figure 3.3.

At the receive end, the sum Y_k is received. The actual transmitted symbol is decoded by subtracting the last received symbol (delayed) from the presently received symbol.

This scheme, however, has the disadvantage that errors once created tend to propagate. This problem can be solved by a precoding technique.

The precoding consists in producing a bit stream for transmission by using the following scheme:

$$b_k = A_k \oplus b_{k-1}$$

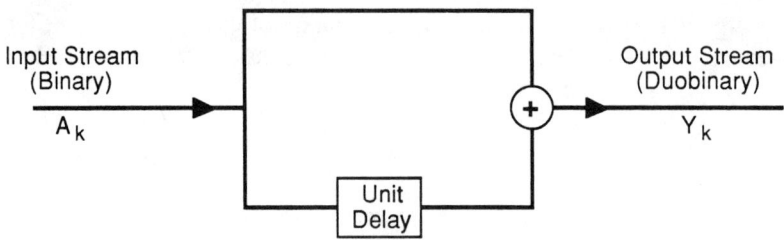

Figure 3.3
Duobinary Encoding Scheme

The symbol ⊕ presents an operation defined as,

$$1 \oplus 1 = 0, \quad 0 \oplus 0 = 0, \quad 1 \oplus 0 = 1, \quad 0 \oplus 1 = 1$$

The precoding technique is shown in Figure 3.4.

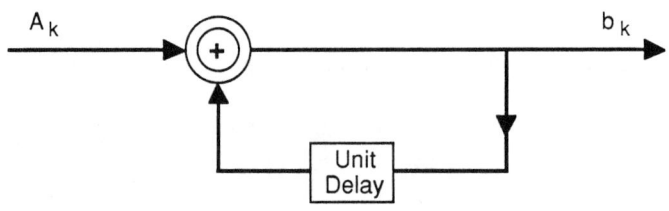

Figure 3.4
Precoding Technique

Using the precoding scheme mentioned above if,

$$A_k = 0, \quad b_k = b_{k-1}$$

$$A_k = 1, \quad b_k = \overline{b_{k-1}}$$

If $+d$ volts were used to transmit the symbol 1, and $-d$ volts to transmit 0, the following rule for decoding will recover the original binary stream:

$$Y_k = \pm 2d \quad \text{implies} \quad A_k = 0$$
$$Y_k = 0 \quad \text{implies} \quad A_k = 1$$

3.1.7 Extensions of Duobinary Transmission Schemes

The duobinary technique can be extended to an L level input. The received samples in this case, being the sum of two consecutive levels, have $2L - 1$ distinct values.

A further generalization can be made by defining the signal Y_k as

$$Y_k = k_0 A_k + k_1 A_{k-1} + k_2 A_{k-2} + \ldots$$

The values and signs of k_i's define the class of coding and the number of terms defines the order n. This is shown in Table 3.1.

Table 3.1
Classes and Orders of Interest*

Classes	k_1	k_2	k_3	k_4	k_5	No. of Rec. Levels
Binary (Ideal)	1					2
1, $n = 2$	1	1				3
2, $n = 3$	1	2	1			5
3, $n = 3$	2	1	−1			5
4, $n = 3$	1	0	−1			3
5, $n = 5$	−1	0	2	0	−1	5

* E. R. Kretzmer, "Generalization of a Technique for Binary Data Communication," IEEE Trans. on Comm. Tech., February 1966, pp. 67-68. © IEEE 1966.

For class 4, $n = 3$, we have

$$Y_k = A_k - A_{k-2}$$

For quaternary input (A_k = 0, 1, 2, 3), Y_k can occupy one of seven levels (−3, −2, −1, 0, 1, 2 and 3).

The major value of the duobinary technique and its generalizations, also called partial response coding schemes, lies in the fact that the frequency spectrum of the resultant signal to be transmitted has characteristics that are better matched to the transmission characteristics of the medium. A study of these characteristics is available in the literature [4].

The class 4, $n = 3$ partial response coding scheme applied to quaternary input has special significance from a practical standpoint. It is used for the Data Under Voice (DUV) scheme used in providing the Dataroute service (Section 1, Reference 2). It has the major advantage of low noise in the low radio baseband frequency region. DUV derives a channel speed of 1.544 Mb/second in the 0-500 kHz baseband region of the frequently used U600 multiplexing scheme in microwave transmission which leaves the baseband vacant below 564 kHz. The justification for choosing the 1.544 Mb/second transmission rate is compatibility with the T1 transmission scheme.

The following example clarifies use of the partial response coding scheme for DUV [5]:

Binary Input (Gray Coded)	10	01	01	00	11	01	00	10	11
Quaternary (A_k)	3	1	1	0	2	1	0	3	2
Precoded (b_k)	3	1	0	1	2	2	2	1	0
Partial Response (Y_k)	3	1	−3	0	2	1	0	−1	−2

The precoding employed here is

$$b_k = A_k \oplus b_{k-2} \text{ modulo } 4$$

Gray coding is used in the quaternary conversion to ensure that a single adjacent level in decoding generates only one bit error.

From the example above it can be seen that the decoder needs to interpret only the negative symbols correctly; the positive symbols are directly decoded as follows:

Y_k	3	2	1	0	−1	−2	−3
A_k	3	2	1	0	3	2	1

A spectral density of the DUV signal using the partial response coding discussed above is shown in [5]. The main virtues of these coding schemes are that they afford relatively simple means of attaining a high transmission efficiency with relatively gentle filter cutoffs, and that one can choose from among a number of differently tapered filter distributions which may be advantageous in specific situations.

3.2 TRANSMISSION MEDIUM FOR DIGITAL SIGNALS

3.2.1 Characteristics

A transmission medium can be characterized in a variety of ways, depending upon the purpose for which the characterization is being carried out. The emphasis in this section will be on those parameters which must be considered in the process of selecting or recommending an appropriate transmission medium for the network.

Figure 3.5 shows a physical transmission medium under consideration here. The transmission medium being considered is in its raw form, that is, without any additional end-to-end enhancement from an error recovery standpoint. A sequence of bits entered at one end of the medium will emerge as a sequence at the other end, each bit suffering a finite, but usually constant, delay and thus maintaining the same order in the output stream as the order in which the bits entered the transmission medium. The transmission medium has no controllable delay or storage associated with it as such; although, depending upon the speed at which data is entering and the end-to-end propagation delay, a certain number of bits will be in transition over the physical medium. As an example, consider the propagation delay between A and B as being 10 milliseconds and the data speed as 1 Megabits per second. At any instant of time, therefore, there are $10^6 \times 10 \times 10^{-3}$ or 10,000 bits in transition over the transmission medium. For a high-speed satellite link (working at, say, 1.5 Megabits per second and a round-trip delay of 600 milliseconds) there will be 900,000 bits in transition in space at any given instant of time.

Two characteristics of a raw transmission medium can be considered. These are: bit sequence independence or bit sequence transparency, and time transparency. The preservation of sequence between the input and the output streams is referred to as the bit sequence independence or bit sequence transparency. Bit sequence transparency does not necessarily imply that each bit suffers the same amount of transition delay. The converse however, is true. If each bit suffers the same amount of transition delay, then bit sequence transparency is guaranteed. Preserving the timing relationship between any two bits in the input stream and the same bits in the output stream is referred to as time transparency. Time transparency implies bit sequence transparency but not vice versa. For the raw transmission medium being considered in this section, both bit sequence and time transparencies hold (See Figure 3.5). This is not necessarily the case when a network is positioned between the end points A and B, as shown in Figure 3.6.

Characterization of the Transmission Medium

The characterization of a raw transmission medium for transporting digital signals can be carried out under the four categories of performance mentioned in Chapter 2, namely,

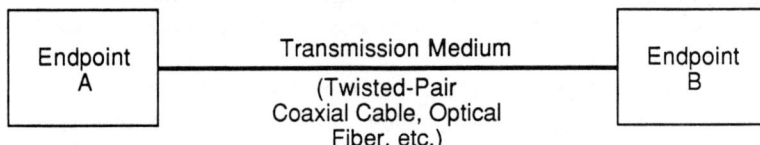

Characteristics

- Bit sequence transparency

- Each signal element suffers a constant delay

Figure 3.5
Characteristics of a Raw Transmission Medium

Characteristics

- Network protocol must be robust to guarantee bit sequence transparency whenever store and forward switching techniques are used

- Networks based on store and forward techniques almost always compromise time transparency

Figure 3.6
Characteristics of a Store and Forward Network

- Delay
- Throughput
- Integrity or accuracy
- Availability

3.2.2 Delay

In the case of a raw transmission medium, delay is usually constant and is equal to the propagation delay. Typical values of propagation delay as a function of distance for different transmission media are furnished in Table 3.2 [6].

Table 3.2
Propagation Delay for Different Transmission Media

Transmission Medium	*Propagation Delay*
Twisted-Pair Copper Wire (2 Mb/sec)	4.3 µsec/km
Coaxial Cable (140 Mb/sec)	3.6 µsec/km
Lightwave Guide (140 Mb/sec)	4.9 µsec/km
Digital Radio (140 Mb/sec)	3.3 µsec/km

3.2.3 Throughput

Throughput of the raw transmission medium is characterized by the maximum speed of data in bits per second that can be sent over it. This is obviously the maximum rate at which information can be transported over the medium. Transmission overheads and channel errors will generally reduce the rate at which actual information is transported over the medium to a value lower than the potential maximum. Throughput is often expressed as a percentage of the nominal channel speed.

The speed of a transmission medium is sometimes referred to in baud. A baud is simply equal to the inverse of the smallest duration of the signal in seconds that could be successfully transmitted over the medium. (The smallest duration of the signal is also sometimes referred to as the unit interval). For example, if the unit interval is 10 milliseconds then the line speed is 100 baud. For specifying the speed of data transmission in baud, the format of the signal itself is unimportant. It may be binary or m-ary (with m distinct levels rather than two). In order to convert baud into bits per second or vice versa, one must know the number of levels associated with each signal element and the probabilities of their occurrence. As shown in Section 3.1, if a signal element could assume m levels, all of which were equally likely, then each element would represent $\log_2 m$ bits of information. If r such signal elements could be transmitted per second, then the throughput of the medium would be $r \log_2 m$ bits per second. As noted in Section 3.1.3, m cannot be indefinitely increased. Its maximum value is limited by the presence of noise and the difficulty associated with discriminating between adjacent levels as m is increased. For the most common case, binary signals, the value of m is 2, that is, throughput in bits per second is equal to the baud rate. This assumes, of course, that there are no overhead elements being transmitted along with the information-bearing elements (see also Section 3.2.3.1).

Sequences of bits that are transmitted over the medium represent symbols, — letters, numerals, special characters, and so on. Depressing a key on a keyboard, say F on an ASCII machine, will cause the following sequence of bits to be transmitted over the line: 10100110. For a table of codes that relates permissible characters to their binary representations, see, for example, [7].

3.2.3.1 Synchronous and Asynchronous Transmission

Let us assume that a certain transmission system is transmitting information at a constant speed, (i.e., a fixed number of units of information per unit of time). For a binary system, this would amount to a fixed number of 1s or 0s per second. The receiving terminal in such a system has to know the speed of transmission in order to detect the incoming bits. Without a knowledge of speed, it will not be able to distinguish a single 1 from a multitude of 1s or a single 0 from a multitude of 0s. Theoretically, then, if the speed is known, the receiver can detect the information bits from the incoming stream. From a practical point of view, however, the receiver has one more problem — determining 'where to look' within a bit time. This need arises because the signals received are likely not perfect, since they may have undergone distortion and been corrupted by noise. The instant at which the receiver is made to look for a 1 or a 0 during the bit duration is chosen so as to minimize the probability of error.

The type of transmission described above, namely, one where information is received at a constant speed all the time, is called Synchronous Transmission. Obviously, in many situations, information does not need to be transmitted continuously. In these cases, the transmitting end remains idle for periods of time. This is called Asynchronous Transmission. There are two ways to handle such situations: (i) Even during the rest period when no effective information is being transmitted, a string of predetermined characters or combination of 1s and 0s is continuously sent. The receiver in this case has to have the capability to notice and detect these idle characters or sequences and discard them. A constant speed of transmission can thus be maintained even through the information to be transmitted is asynchronous. (ii) The transmitter and the receiver are brought to a complete halt until the next transmission requirement arises. The start of transmission initiates a fresh string of information bits on the line and the receiver interprets them as received.

Obviously, the asynchronous information transmission requirement can be served by a synchronous transmission system. An obvious requirement, of course, is that the information for transmission be generated at a rate lower than the speed of the transmission medium.

In all data transmission systems, the receiver is required to track the transmitter (i.e., attain the state of the transmitter) after a period of time called the transmission delay. Provision must be made to guard against mistracks caused by errors, omissions, or repetitions and to subsequently reinitialize the receiver. (You can imagine the frustrations in interpreting a message in which each alphabet, including space, is represented by eight bits and one of the bits is missed or repeated in the transmission process).

The actual transmission process, therefore, requires a little more organization. In 'character-at-a-time' or asynchronous transmission systems, each character is preceded by a start bit. The start and stop bits are complementary, so that there is no chance of mixing up two characters. Further, the stop bit can be made of arbitrary length until the next character has to be transmitted. In this simple system there is no systematic buildup of error due to the differing speeds of the clocks of the receiver and the transmitter. The system is rugged, although it is so at the cost of high overheads.

A simple and logical extension of the above scheme is transmission on a block or frame basis. Rather than sending special bits with each character, a number of characters could be grouped together for transmission and preceded and succeeded by a special string of bits which the receiver is capable of recognizing. The size of the frame or block can be fixed or variable, depending upon the particular application and the transmission environment.

3.2.3.2 Numerical Examples

We will illustrate several points of importance that are related to asynchronous or character-by-character transmission through the following examples:

Example 1: A teletypewriter makes use of a 5-bit code, each bit being 14.5 milliseconds in length. A single character consists of a start pulse and the five information pulses, each of 14.5 milliseconds duration. A stop pulse of 20 milliseconds ends the character.

What is the rate 'of information' transmission in bits per second and the signaling rate in baud? If a lapse period of 25 milliseconds is arbitrarily inserted between two characters, how are the information transmission rate in bits per second and the signaling rate in baud affected?

Solution: In Section 3.2.3 we defined baud rate as being equal to the inverse of the duration (in seconds) of the smallest single element. Using this definition, the baud rate is equal to $1/14.5 \times 10^{-3}$ or 68.96 baud.

Bit speed depends on the number of information bits transmitted per second. In the example, in order to transmit 5 information bits, we must transmit on the line: one start pulse of 14.5 milliseconds duration, five information bits of 5×14.5 or 72.5 milliseconds duration and one stop bit of 20 milliseconds duration.

Therefore, five information bits take a total of $14.5 + 72.5 + 20 = 107$ milliseconds, making the speed in bits per second equal to $5/107 \times 10^{-3}$ or 46.72 bits per second.

If a lapse of 25 milliseconds is introduced between the stop pulse of one character and the start pulse of another, the new bit rate is $5/132 \times 10^{-3}$ or 37.87 bits per second. The baud rate remains unchanged since the duration of the smallest signal element on the line is not affected.

Example 2: As another example, consider a quaternary synchronous transmission system of the following description:

Number of distinct levels = 4

Duration of each signal element = 1 millisecond

The baud rate of the system is 1000 but the information transmission rate in bits per second is now equal to $\log_2 4/10^{-3}$ or 2000 bits per second.

3.2.4 Integrity or Accuracy

Integrity of transmission is an indicator of the accuracy of the transmission process. A distribution of bit errors can completely characterize the transmission process. If the bits in error were randomly distributed, the probability of a bit being in error or the bit error rate (BER) would be a useful parameter and could be used for completely characterizing the transmission medium in a statistically predictable manner.

Unfortunately, the distribution of bit errors is seldom random or in conformity to simple statistical distributions. This makes it necessary to choose the right parameter or the set of right parameters for the specific purpose at hand. We address this question more fully in Chapter 5.

3.2.5 Availability [8,9,10]

The availability of a transmission medium (in general, of any system) is the probability that it is operational. It is often expressed as a percentage. Availability* can be calculated as:

$$\text{Availability } A = \frac{\text{MTBF}}{\text{MTBF} + \text{MTTR}} \quad (3.8)$$

where

MTBF = Mean time between failures

MTTR = Mean time to repair a failure

Equation (3.8) can also be written as:

$$\text{Availability } A = \frac{\text{Up Time}}{\text{Up Time} + \text{Down Time}} \quad (3.9)$$

The denominator in Equation (3.9) represents the total period of observation.

Availabilities of typical transmission media are furnished in Table 3.3.

System Reliability is often used to express a similar notion. The reliability $R(t)$ of a system is defined as the probability that the system will operate successfully (with no failures occurring) in the time interval (0,t). The reliability function is often expressed as an exponential function as:

$$R(t) = e^{-\lambda t} \quad (3.10)$$

From Equation (3.10), the failure density function can be derived as [8]:

$$f(t) = \lambda e^{-\lambda t} \quad (3.11)$$

---

* We are considering here only the average or limiting availability. In actual fact, availability is a random variable. For example, if availability is measured using actual field data, it will vary from year to year.

Table 3.3
Availabilities of Typical Transmission Media

Transmission Medium	Availability (%)
Local Loop	99.99
DDS Channel	99.96
Satellite Channel*	99.96
Private Line (4 kHz) (100 miles) [10]	97.50

* J. Martin, *Communications Satellite Systems*, Prentice-Hall Inc., Englewood Cliffs, N.J., 1978, Chapter 23.

The mean time between failure, MTBF, can now be expressed as:

$$\text{MTBF} = \int_0^\infty t f(t) dt$$

$$= \int_0^\infty t \lambda e^{-\lambda t} dt$$

$$= \left[-t e^{-\lambda t} \right]_0^\infty - \left[\frac{-e^{-\lambda t}}{\lambda} \right]_0^\infty$$

$$= \frac{1}{\lambda} \tag{3.12}$$

The parameter λ is termed the failure rate of the system.

An identical concept is used to describe the maintainability of a system. The maintainability function is often expressed as:

$$M(t) = e^{-\mu t} \tag{3.13}$$

It can be shown, as above, that,

$$\text{MTTR} = \frac{1}{\mu} \tag{3.14}$$

The parameter μ is termed the repair rate of the system.

Using Equations (3.12) and (3.14), we have, for the exponentially distributed reliability and maintainability functions, the Availability A expressed as:

$$A = \frac{\frac{1}{\lambda}}{\frac{1}{\lambda} + \frac{1}{\mu}} = \frac{\mu}{\lambda + \mu} \tag{3.15}$$

Notice that Equation (3.15) holds only for the specific case when the reliability and maintainability functions are exponential.

From a user's point of view, it is not always practical to distinguish between complete failure of a transmission medium and a period of high bit error rate. The CCITT position is that if the error rate exceeds 10^{-3} in each second for more than ten consecutive seconds, a complete failure is deemed to have occurred, resulting in an unavailability condition [11].

The importance of the manner in which the durations of outages are distributed cannot be overemphasized. Obviously, if the maintainability function is exponentially distributed, the durations of outages can be statistically predicted. This knowledge is essential in computing user-level performance and, in particular, in designing a system that meets users' needs.

J. D. Markov et al [10] have derived a general model for a randomly selected 2400-bits-per-second telephone line between two points. Figure 3.7 shows all the disturbances that occur to cause unacceptable operation of this line. These disturbances, regardless of their cause, consist of a set of failure events that vary in time. Figure 3.7 plots these failure events on the abscissa of a logarithmic scale to include the large range of values considered.

The minimum length of a failure or disturbance that is relevant to a transmission rate of 2400 bits per second is 1/2400 seconds or 42 milliseconds. The length of the duration of the failure is varied continuously from the duration of one bit to several days. For each duration of failure, the mean time between failure is observed and plotted on the ordinate.

It can be observed from Figure 3.7 that errors of a single bit or 42 milliseconds duration occur once every 40 seconds, which corresponds to a bit error rate of 1 in 10^5. Errors of one minute duration occur about once per day. A one-hour disturbance can be expected each month and disturbances lasting one day occur once each year.

Figure 3.7 is by no means a general characterization of telephone lines. It has been included here to present a general perspective on error events and their durations on the same graph. Usually, errors of shorter and longer durations are presented separately, as they affect system performance and influence system design in different ways. This is discussed in Chapter 4.

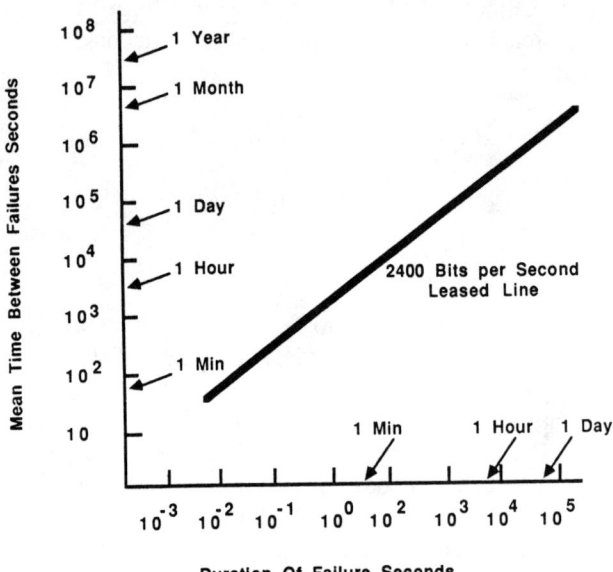

Figure 3.7
Mean Time Between Failures vs. Outage Duration*

3.2.5.1 An Example

Consider the end-to-end computer communication network structure shown in Figure 2.1. In this configuration if either of the access subsystems or the network fails, the user will experience an overall system failure. If we assume that the failure characteristics of each of the three components of the end-to-end system are statistically independent, then the availability of the end-to-end system can be expressed as:

$$A = A_1 A_2 A_3 \qquad (3.16)$$

where A_1, A_2 and A_3 are the availabilities of the terminal-access subsystem, the network, and the host-access subsystem, respectively. Equation (3.16) easily follows from the independence assumptions.

---

* J. D. Markov, M. W. Doss and S. A. Mitchell, "A Reliability Model for Data Communications," Proc. Int. Conf. Comm. ICC-78, Toronto, June 1978, pp. 3.4.1-3.4.5 © IEEE 1978.

Given $A_1 = A_3 = .9996$

$A_2 = .990$

the end-to-end availability can be easily computed as

$$A = A_1 A_2 A_3$$

$$= .9892 \text{ or } 98.92\%$$

3.3 REFERENCES

[1] C. E. Shannon and W. Weaver, *The Mathematical Theory of Communication*, University of Illinois Press, Urbana, 1949.

[2] *Datapro Report on Data Communications*, Datapro Research Corporation, Vol. 3, March 1986.

[3] R. W. Lucky, J. Salz, and E. J. Weldon, Jr., *Principles of Data Communications*, McGraw-Hill, New York, 1968.

[4] E. R. Kretzmer, "Generalization of a Technique for Binary Data Communication," IEEE Trans. on Comm. Tech., February 1966, pp. 67-68.

[5] D. M. Baker, "Analog/Digital Hybrid Radio Uses Vacant Baseband," Canadian Electronics Engineering, February 1973, pp. 34-37.

[6] R. W. McLintock, "Overview of International Standards for Transmission Impairments Affecting Digital Telecommunication Networks," Computer Networks and ISDN Systems, Vol. 9, No. 5, May 1985, pp. 339-344.

[7] A. Ralston, Ed., *Encyclopedia of Computer Science*, Petrocelli/Charter, New York, 1976, p. 121.

[8] B. S. Dhillon and C. Singh, *Engineering Reliability*, J. Wiley, New York, 1981, Chapter 3.

[9] A. Trivedi, C. Bedard, and N. Gibbs, "Reliability and Availability Design Considerations in Datapac," Proc. Int. Conf. Comm. ICC-78, Toronto, June 1978, pp. 3.2.1-3.2.5.

[10] J. D. Markov, M. W. Doss and S. A. Mitchell, "A Reliability Model for Data Communications," Proc. Int. Conf. Comm. ICC-78, Toronto, June 1978, pp. 3.4.1-3.4.5.

[11] CCITT Recommendations, G.821, *Error Performance on an International Digital Connection Forming Part of an ISDN*, *Red Book* (1984).

Chapter 4

NETWORK STATES AND HIERARCHIES OF PERFORMANCE

This chapter distinguishes between the two states of a network — operational or nonoperational — from a user's standpoint. It also introduces the concept of a hierarchical manner in which the overall performance of a network can be viewed. This approach will bring out the factors which affect the overall performance as perceived by a user and the relationship among these factors from a performance standpoint.

4.1 THE OPERATIONAL AND NONOPERATIONAL STATES OF A SYSTEM

A user may view a network as being either operational or nonoperational. During its operational state, a network meets its functional and performance requirements. In a nonoperational state, either the network fails to meet its functional requirements, or its performance falls below the threshold of acceptability. The nonoperational state of a network is also referred to as an outage or an unavailability condition. The transition from an operational or to a nonoperational state may be abrupt or smooth. Obviously, from a user's perspective, a smooth transition is far more desirable than an abrupt one. A smooth transition will result in a predictable status at recovery and will, for example, alert a user to a lost transaction so as to remove or minimize the uncertainty concerning the response received at the far end.

The transition from a nonoperational state to an operational one may be automatic or may require manual intervention. From a user's perspective, the difference between manual and automatic transition may be insignificant except as to their relative durations. However, from a network provider's perspective, this difference is quite significant. Those restorations to normalcy that require human intervention have to be planned for in conjunction with manpower availability constraints. Obviously, it is important to ensure that delays encountered solely in the process of locating manpower and/or the appropriate replacement subsystem(s) do not significantly alter the outage characteristics of the network.

How does a user detect that a network is nonoperational? A system's failure to meet the functional requirements anticipated can indicate an outage condition. Alternatively, persistent degradation of one or more performance parameters beyond the threshold of acceptability will also make the network unusable and, therefore, unavailable. Different sets of performance parameters are, in general, applicable to different application environments. It is thus entirely possible that a network is available for one class of applications but not available for another class. For example, consider a computer communication network whose internodal links are comprised of both terrestrial and satellite channels. If the low-delay terrestrial links are down, the network is unsuitable for short inquiry-response applications. However, it may still be suitable for carrying on remote job entry applications.

4.2 NETWORK BEHAVIOR DURING AN OPERATIONAL STATE

When a network is operational, it may be entirely free from errors (or malfunctions), or it may be subject to occasional or systematic errors. All systems are designed to handle and recuperate gracefully from occasional errors. Occasional errors in transmission are usually corrected so that they are effectively hidden from the end user. For certain applications characterized by high redundancy, however, it may be acceptable to pass occasional errors on to the end user. Occasional errors are usually traceable to probabilistic error behavior of transmission lines or electronic circuits. Their occurrences can be predicted only statistically.

Systematic errors are caused by events such as resynchronization, booting, and so on, where a network subsystem, in response to a detected (and persistent) malfunction, starts executing a programmed routine. Systematic errors, if not recovered from within a brief time consistent with the application, may lead to a nonoperational state. Alternatively, some kinds or patterns of systematic errors may be classified as leading the network to a nonoperational state as soon as detected.

It may not be always possible to distinguish between systematic errors and a combination of random errors with similar characteristics. Between the clearly separable cases of occasional errors and systematic errors, there must necessarily be a class of errors that do not clearly fall into one or the other category. A network must be able to deal effectively with the entire spectrum of error behavior.

One important aspect of network performance is the determination of when it has gone into a nonoperational state. When such a situation is detected, the network must immediately communicate its 'unavailable' status to the end users. The end-user machines must be capable of recognizing the special unavailability response and in turn must discard any data received during the outage period and refrain from entrusting new data to the network.

It should be understood that each type of error or unavailability behavior has different implications for different applications. Some applications can tolerate occasional errors rather well, while others may be quite sensitive to them. Similarly, some applications can live with a series of well-spaced outages of small duration much better than with a single outage of longer duration.

4.3 COMPUTER COMMUNICATION NETWORKS

4.3.1 A Hierarchical View

The functional elements of most networks are organized in a number of layers which are hierarchically structured. Layering provides a number of advantages to the designer as well as to the user. Each layer provides a well-defined set of services to the higher layer, the overall design problem is thus broken down into the more manageable one of designing of smaller subsets of functions. From the user's perspective, great flexibility can be realized if the layers and their functions are standardized across a number of networks and subsystems providing the standardized functions are available from a number of vendors.

4.3.2 The ISO/CCITT Layered Model

In 1978, the International Standards Organization (ISO) recognized that standards for networks of heterogeneous systems were required and initiated an activity known as Open System Interconnection (OSI). The OSI reference model provides a layered architecture effectively breaking up the overall problem of machine-to-machine communication into manageable pieces. The reference model is an abstract model; adherence to the model by two different systems does not by itself guarantee effective communication between them. The OSI service specifications and the OSI protocol specifications successively tighten up the abstractions, with the protocol specifications representing the lowest level of abstraction. Two open systems may have different implementations, but identical protocol specifications within the OSI framework will allow them to communicate with each other. There are seven different layers in the proposed OSI reference model. At the present time, protocol specifications for the lowest five levels (levels one through five) have been agreed upon by the responsible ISO committees and work on the higher levels is in progress. The interested reader is referred to a special issue of the proceedings of the IEEE addressing the different aspects of the OSI architecture and protocols [1].

4.3.3 A Hierarchical Performance Model

It is possible and indeed convenient to look upon the end-to-end performance of a computer communication network in a structured fashion as well. Such a performance structure can closely follow the network's layered design structure. Performance limitations (or enhancements) provided by each layer can be assessed separately as well as in conjunction with other layers. The end-to-end performance can be derived from a knowledge of the performance of each of the layers.

The lowest layer — Layer 1 — provides a physical transmission medium. Examples of transmission media are metallic wires, open air using radio or microwaves, satellite channels, or lightwave guides. The performance characteristics of a transmission medium, discussed fully in Chapter 5, are referred to as the transmission-level performance.

The next layer — the Link Layer — is created by introducing a protocol between two end points communicating over a physical transmission medium. The link layer protocol ensures the integrity of transmission on a point-to-point basis. Performance implications of link-level protocols are examined in Chapter 6. Enhanced performance due to the use of a link layer protocol is referred to as communication-level performance. Chapter 7 addresses the question of end-to-end performance in a packet switched network.

In this book we limit our discussion of performance up to and including the packet level. It is hoped, however, that the techniques used for analysis here can be extended to higher levels, eventually encompassing the performance aspects of two applications communicating to each other.

4.4 REFERENCE

[1] Proceedings of the IEEE, Special Issue on Open Systems Interconnection, December 1983.

Chapter 5

TRANSMISSION-LEVEL PERFORMANCE

This chapter will introduce the parameters in terms of which the integrity or accuracy of transmission can be assessed. Relationships between the different parameters are derived and explained.

5.1 CHARACTERIZATION OF TRANSMISSION ACCURACY

I now introduce the parameters in terms of which the integrity or accuracy of transmission is usually assessed and presented. We are considering here a transmission medium in its raw form, that is, without any additional enhancements on an end-to-end basis. A characterization of the performance of the raw transmission medium is also termed transmission-level performance. In the next chapter, we shall see how the use of suitable error correction techniques can enhance transmission-level performance so that inaccuracies of transmission are effectively hidden from the user.

I stated in Chapter 1 that enhancement of performance can usually be carried out by incurring additional costs. Physically, transmission-level performance can be improved using different techniques depending upon the transmission medium under consideration. Some examples of such potential improvements are: reducing repeater or regenerator spacings, enhancing carrier power level, reducing interference from external sources, and so on.

A question that may come to mind is: To what extent is it desirable to carry out such improvements, or alternatively, What is the optimum transmission-level performance for a transmission medium? In order to answer this question from an engineering perspective, one has to define two parameters — value and cost — and determine their relationship. Value is related to the function the user is engaged in; for example, parameters like throughput or delay can be used as values. Chapter 8 considers the general question of performance objectives and how they can be derived. In general, performance objectives are goals which have been identified using some criteria of optimality.

5.2 BIT ERROR RATE

For a transmission medium conveying information in a digital format, bit error statistics provide the finest or the lowest level of detail necessary in selecting a transmission medium. Bit error rate (BER) is one of several possible parameters at the bit level, all of which might together represent bit error statistics. BER is defined as:

$$\text{BER} = \frac{\{\text{Number of bits received in error}\}}{\{\text{Total number of bits received}\}} \quad (5.1)$$

If the distribution of bits in error is random, a knowledge of the BER is sufficient to characterize the transmission medium on a statistical basis. However, most of the time this is not the case, and bits in error tend to occur in bursts. In comparison to random errors, bursty errors may have a substantially different effect on the degradation perceived by the user, even though the BER may be identical in both cases.

Consider a user transmitting information at 4800 bits per second synchronously. Further, let the information be organized in 8-bit characters such that 600 characters are nominally transmitted each second. Let the probability of each bit being in error be the same (i.e., let the distribution of bits in error be random). Assume the BER to be .0001. Then the probability of a bit being received correctly is $(1 - .0001)$ or .9999. The probability that all the bits in a character are received correctly is equal to $(1 - .0001)^8$ and the probability that there is at least one error in a character, or the character error rate (CER), is equal to

$$1 - (1 - .0001)^8 = .0008$$

The above example indicates that even though, on the average, one bit in 10,000 bits is received erroneously, the ratio of characters received in error is substantially higher (i.e., 1 in 1250).

To the user who is transmitting information on a character-by-character basis, the ratio of characters received in error is far more important than the bit error rate associated with the transmission medium. Now suppose that the distribution of bits in error is nonrandom and that errors tend to occur in bursts, while the BER is still 1 in 10,000. What will be the effect of this type of bit error distribution on the character error rate?

Since we have now assumed that the bits in error are occurring in bursts, the probability that a character in error has more than one bit in error is higher than in the random case. If the average number of bits in error over a long stream of bits is the same in both cases, it follows that the nonrandom case has a larger number of error-free characters than the random case. The residual throughput (i.e., the error-free character transmission rate) in the nonrandom case is thus higher than in the random case. A transmission medium with a nonrandom error distribution is thus more desirable than one with a random error distribution of identical BER from a throughput point of view. However, there may be other factors to consider and the sole use of this criterion in the selection of a transmission medium may be misleading in some cases. For example, random errors are usually easier to cope with for most applications. Long bursts of error may lead to unavailability conditions, resulting in additional delays due to, say, reinitialization of the whole or parts of the system. For an on-line system a long outage, however infrequent, may simply be unacceptable.

5.3 BLOCK TRANSMISSION

5.3.1 Block Error Rate

Synchronous transmission between two terminals over a physical transmission medium is most often carried out in a block format. This means that a chain of information bits consisting of several characters is identified with a beginning and an end and transmitted as a block. The primary purpose of block oriented transmission is the ability to detect block errors, leading to their correction by retransmission of the entire block.

A block is declared to be in error if one or more bits are detected to be in error in the whole block. The block error rate will always be higher than the bit error rate or the character error rate, its magnitude depending upon the transmission environment and the block size. For block oriented transmission, the block error rate is meaningfully related to the throughput observed by the user. We use the following example to illustrate the evaluation of block error rates.

5.3.2 An Example

Transactions consisting of 100 five-bit characters are to be sent over sub-voice-grade lines. What is the probability that a received message will have an error in it? Assume a bit error rate of 1 in 10^4. Bits in error are randomly distributed.

Let

$$P = \text{probability of error in a transaction}$$

and

$$p = \text{probability of a bit in error or BER}$$

Then

$$P = 1 - (1 - p)^n \qquad (5.2)$$

where

$$n = \text{number of bits in a transaction, i.e., } n = 500$$

Equation (5.2) follows from the discussions in Section 5.2.

From Equation (5.2), using the given values for p and n, we have,

$$P = 1 - (1 - .0001)^{500}$$

$$\approx 1 - (1 - .0001 \times 500)$$

$$= .0001 \times 500 = .05 = 1/20$$

This means that, on the average, one transaction in twenty transactions will be in error.

5.4 ERROR-FREE INTERVAL

5.4.1 Mean Error-Free Interval

We have seen earlier in this chapter that efficient transmission of data depends both on the exact structure of the error pattern and the BER. While traditionally BER has been used as the sole criterion to characterize transmission of digital signals, additional parameters such as the Mean Error-

Free Interval (MEFI) have also been introduced to further qualify a transmission medium [1,2].

Consider a data string of N bits composed of blocks of length L bits each, including any overhead. This string of bits is being transmitted over a random error medium with a BER equal to p. As discussed earlier, a block will be considered to be in error when at least one of its bits is in error. The Error-Free Interval (EFI) is defined as the number of consecutive error-free blocks between two blocks in error. Our objective, then, is to evaluate the Mean Error-Free Interval (MEFI) in blocks.

5.4.2 MEFI Knowing i Blocks in Error [3]

We will first calculate the MEFI assuming that out of the B (= N/L) blocks, we know that i blocks are in error, $i = 0, 1, 2, \ldots, B$.

There are $\binom{B}{i}$ possible arrangements of the i error blocks among the total B. In those $\binom{B}{i}$ combinations, we observe various EFIs of length K ranging from 1 to $B - i$. The following result will be proved.

Proposition 1: The number of EFIs of length K blocks is given by:

$$N(K) = (i + 1) \binom{B - K - 1}{i - 1}, \quad K = 1, 2, \ldots, B - i \tag{5.3}$$

Proof: An EFI of length K may occur at either (1) one of the ends of the data string, or (2) the interior of the data string.

In case (1) the EFIs of length K blocks have the patterns shown in Figure 5.1.

The number of those patterns is equal to the number of combinations of the remaining $(i - 1)$ error-blocks in $(B - K - 1)$ positions, that is,

$$2 \binom{B - K - 1}{i - 1} \tag{5.4}$$

The pattern of EFIs of type 2 is shown in Figure 5.2, and their number is equal to the number of combinations of the remaining $(i - 2)$ errors in $(B - K - 2)$ positions, that is,

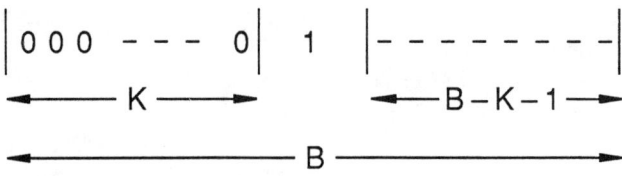

1: Block in error
0: Error-free block

Figure 5.1
An Error Free Interval of Length K at One of the Ends*

$$(B - K - 1) \begin{bmatrix} B - K - 2 \\ i - 2 \end{bmatrix} \quad (5.5)$$

Therefore, the total number of EFIs of length K is:

$$N(K) = 2 \begin{bmatrix} B - K - 1 \\ i - 1 \end{bmatrix} + (B - K - 1) \begin{bmatrix} B - K - 2 \\ i - 2 \end{bmatrix}$$

$$= (i + 1) \begin{bmatrix} B - K - 1 \\ i - 1 \end{bmatrix} \quad (5.6)$$

We can now compute the conditional MEFI. The result is surprisingly simple.

Proposition 2: The Mean Error-Free Interval, given that i blocks out of B are in error, is:

---

* P. K. Verma, S. G. S. Shiva, N. D. Georganas, and J. S. Jawanda, "Evaluation of the Mean Error-Free Interval of a Noisy Data Channel," IEEE Trans. on Comm., Vol. Com-26, No. 1, January 1978, pp. 185-187 © IEEE 1980.

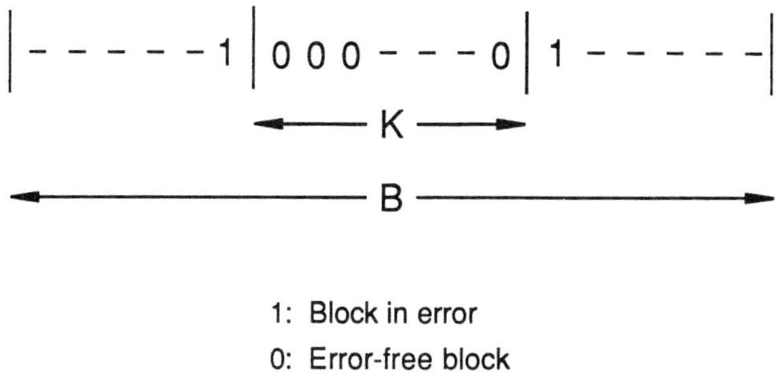

Error-Free Interval

```
|------1|0 0 0 ---0|1------|
        ←— K —→
←————————— B —————————→
```

1: Block in error
0: Error-free block

Figure 5.2
An Error Free Interval of Length K in the Interior*

$$\text{MEFI}\big|_i = \frac{B}{i+1} \quad \text{for } i = 0, 1, \ldots, B-1 \tag{5.7}$$

$$= 0 \text{ for } i = B$$

Proof:

First, for $i < B$,

$$\text{MEFI}\big|_i = \sum_{K=1}^{B-i} KN(K) \Big/ \sum_{K=1}^{B-i} N(K) = \sum_{K=1}^{B-i} K \binom{B-K-1}{i-1} \Big/ \sum_{K=1}^{B-i} \binom{B-K-1}{i-1}$$

We compute separately the denominator and numerator of the above expression making use of the combinatorial identity

$$\binom{n+1}{m} = \binom{n}{m} + \binom{n-1}{m-1} + \ldots + \binom{n-m}{0} \quad \text{for } n \leq m, \tag{5.8}$$

---

* P. K. Verma, S. G. S. Shiva, N. D. Georganas, and J. S. Jawanda, "Evaluation of the Mean Error-Free Interval of a Noisy Data Channel," IEEE Trans. on Comm., Vol. Com-26, No. 1, January 1978, pp. 185-187 © IEEE 1980.

Now,

$$\sum_{K=1}^{B-i} \begin{bmatrix} B-K-1 \\ i-1 \end{bmatrix} = \sum_{k=1}^{B-i} \begin{bmatrix} B-K-1 \\ B-K-i \end{bmatrix}$$

$$= \begin{bmatrix} B-2 \\ B-i-1 \end{bmatrix} + \begin{bmatrix} B-3 \\ B-i-2 \end{bmatrix} + \ldots + \begin{bmatrix} i-1 \\ 0 \end{bmatrix}$$

$$= \begin{bmatrix} B-1 \\ B-i-1 \end{bmatrix} = \begin{bmatrix} B-1 \\ i \end{bmatrix} \qquad (5.9)$$

and

$$\sum_{K=1}^{B-i} K \begin{bmatrix} B-K-1 \\ i-1 \end{bmatrix} = \sum_{K=1}^{B-i} K \begin{bmatrix} B-K-1 \\ B-K-i \end{bmatrix}$$

$$= \begin{bmatrix} B-2 \\ B-i-1 \end{bmatrix} + 2 \begin{bmatrix} B-3 \\ B-i-2 \end{bmatrix} + \ldots + (B-i) \begin{bmatrix} i-1 \\ 0 \end{bmatrix}$$

$$= \begin{bmatrix} B-2 \\ B-i-1 \end{bmatrix} + \begin{bmatrix} B-3 \\ B-i-2 \end{bmatrix} + \ldots + \begin{bmatrix} i-1 \\ 0 \end{bmatrix} +$$

$$+ \begin{bmatrix} B-3 \\ B-i-2 \end{bmatrix} + \ldots + \begin{bmatrix} i-1 \\ 0 \end{bmatrix} + \ldots + \begin{bmatrix} i-1 \\ 0 \end{bmatrix}$$

$$= \begin{bmatrix} B-1 \\ B-i-1 \end{bmatrix} + \begin{bmatrix} B-2 \\ B-i-2 \end{bmatrix} + \ldots + \begin{bmatrix} i-1 \\ 0 \end{bmatrix}$$

$$= \begin{bmatrix} B \\ B-i-1 \end{bmatrix} = \begin{bmatrix} B \\ i+1 \end{bmatrix} \qquad (5.10)$$

Error-Free Interval

Therefore:

$$\text{MEFI}\Big|_i = \begin{bmatrix} B \\ i+1 \end{bmatrix} \Big/ \begin{bmatrix} B-1 \\ i \end{bmatrix} = \frac{B}{i+1} \; ; i = 1, 2, \ldots, B-1$$

Clearly for $i = B$, $\text{MEFI}\Big|_i = 0$.

It is to be noted here that the above results for the conditional Error-Free Interval are independent of the type of channel and thus, valid not only for the random-error channel, but for any type of channel noise.

Concentrating now on the random-error channel, we can calculate the unconditional MEFI.

First, the probability of a block being in error, that is, having at least one bit in error, is clearly:

$$P = 1 - (1 - p)^L \tag{5.11}$$

where p is the BER.

The probability of i blocks being in error is given by the binomial distribution

$$P\Big|_i = \begin{bmatrix} B \\ i \end{bmatrix} P^i (1 - P)^{B-i} \tag{5.12}$$

The following proposition gives the unconditional MEFI

Proposition 3: In a data string of B blocks, the Mean Error-Free Interval, measured in block lengths, is:

$$\text{MEFI} = \frac{B}{(B+1)P} [1 - P^B + 1 - (1-P)^B + 1] \tag{5.13}$$

Proof:

$$\text{MEFI} = \sum_{i=0}^{B} \Big[\text{MEFI}\Big|_i\Big] P\Big|_i = \sum_{i=0}^{B-1} \frac{B}{i+1} \begin{bmatrix} B \\ i \end{bmatrix} P^i (1-P)^{B-i}$$

$$= \frac{B}{(B+1)P} \sum_{i=0}^{B-1} \binom{B+1}{i+1} P^{i+1}(1-P)^{B-i}$$

$$= \frac{B}{(B+1)P} \sum_{j=1}^{B} \binom{B+1}{j} P^{j} (1-P)^{B+1-j}$$

$$= \frac{B}{(B+1)P} [1-P^{B+1} - (1-P)^{B+1}].$$

Remark: Relation (5.13) is also valid for non random-error channels wherever (5.12) is valid, i.e., where the blocks in error are statistically independent.

A case of practical interest arises when the data string is very long, i.e., $B \rightarrow \infty$. Taking the limit in equation (5.13) we obtain the following result:

Corollary: For a very long data string, the Mean Error-Free Interval, measured in blocks is given by:

$$MEFI = \frac{1}{P} \; ; \text{ for } P < 1$$

$$= 0 \; ; \text{ for } P = 1 \qquad (5.14)$$

The apparent discontinuity of $MEFI\big|_{B \rightarrow \infty}$, as a function of the block error rate P, and at P=1, can easily be explained. If $P = 1$, all blocks are in error and thus $MEFI\big|_{B \rightarrow \infty} = 0$. But if, for example P=0.9999, and B=∞, 1 packet out of every 10,000 is error-free, thus the MEFI is close to the value $1/P \simeq 1$ which is near 0 on a scale with large L's.

From equations (5.11) and (5.14), we obtain,

$$MEFI\big|_{B \rightarrow \infty} = \frac{1}{1 - (1-p)^L} \qquad (5.15)$$

which gives the Mean Error-Free Interval, as a function of the Bit Error Rate and of the block length, measured in bits. Figure 5.3 shows the plot of $MEFI\big|_{B \rightarrow \infty}$ vs L, for various BER p's.

Error-Free Interval

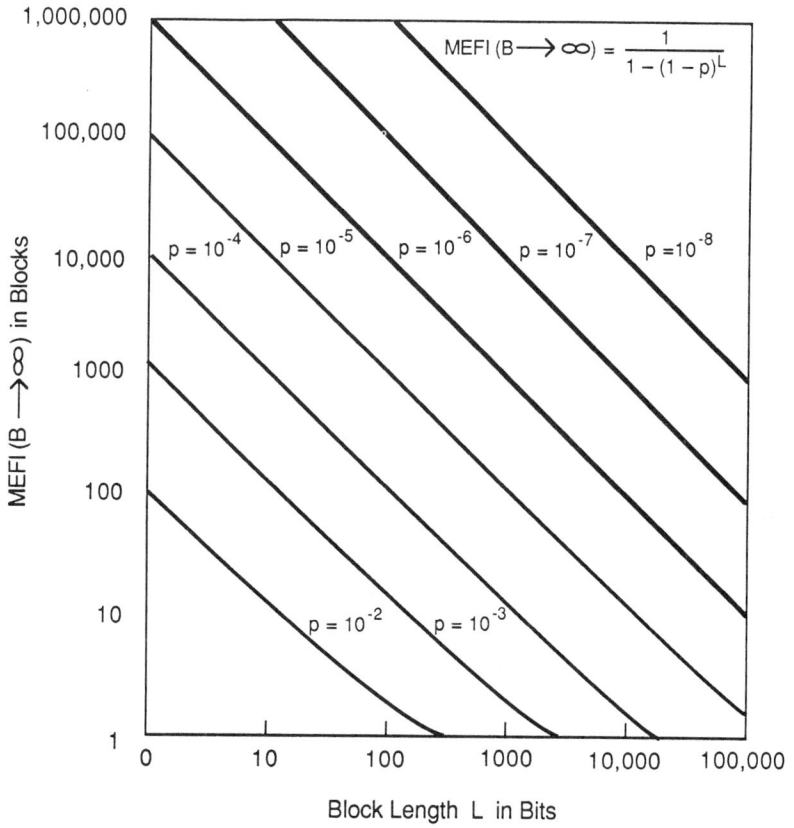

Figure 5.3
MEFI ($B \to \infty$) vs L*

If R bits/sec is the data rate, we can obtain the value of MEFI in sec from Equation (5.14) as:

$$MEFI\Big|_{B \to \infty} = \frac{L/R}{1 - (1-p)^L} \quad \text{seconds.} \quad (5.16)$$

---

* P. K. Verma, S. G. S. Shiva, N. D. Georganas, and J. S. Jawanda, "Evaluation of the Mean Error-Free Interval of a Noisy Data Channel," IEEE Trans. on Comm., Vol. Com-26, No. 1, January 1978, pp. 185-187 © IEEE 1980.

5.5 ERROR-FREE SECONDS

Transmission performance is sometimes specified in terms of Error-Free Seconds, usually expressed as a percentage of total seconds of transmission (% EFS) over a period of time. One second is a period of observation here and seconds with one or more bit errors are classified as error seconds, while those without any error are classified as error-free seconds. Clearly,

$$\% \text{ EFS} = \frac{\text{Total error-free seconds}}{\text{Total seconds of transmission}} \qquad (5.17)$$

For blocks equivalent to one second of transmission time, such as, 4800-bit blocks being transmitted at 4800 bits per second, % EFS is related to the block error rate by the simple relationship,

$$\% \text{ EFS} = 1 - (\text{Block Error Rate}) \qquad (5.18)$$

The main advantage of % EFS in characterizing the error performance of a transmission medium lies in the simplicity with which it can be interpreted. One can increase or reduce the one-second period (the period of observation), and propose parameters higher than a second (such as a deca-second) or lower than a second (such as a deci-second) instead. If the period of observation is equal to the block length in bits, divided by the transmission speed in bits per second, one would get a relationship between % EFS and the block error rate similar to that in Equation (5.18).

If the period of observation is larger, then

$$\% \text{ Error-Free Periods} < 1 - \text{Block Error Rate}$$

and conversely, for periods of observation that are smaller than the block length expressed in time,

$$\% \text{ Error-Free Periods} > 1 - \text{Block Error Rate}$$

There are limits to increasing or reducing the period of observation. Beyond these limits, its usefulness as a transmission-level performance parameter is significantly reduced. A gradual reduction in the period of observation will result in the error rate being assessed in terms of a lower (proportionately reduced) number of bits in each period. Eventually, when the period of observation becomes one bit, the bit error rate and the block error rate are identical. A similar conclusion can be derived as the block length or the period of observation is increased. As the block length is increased, the block error rate increases, asymptotically reaching unity. For a specific BER of 10^{-5}, the relationship between block error rate and block length is shown in Figure 5.4.

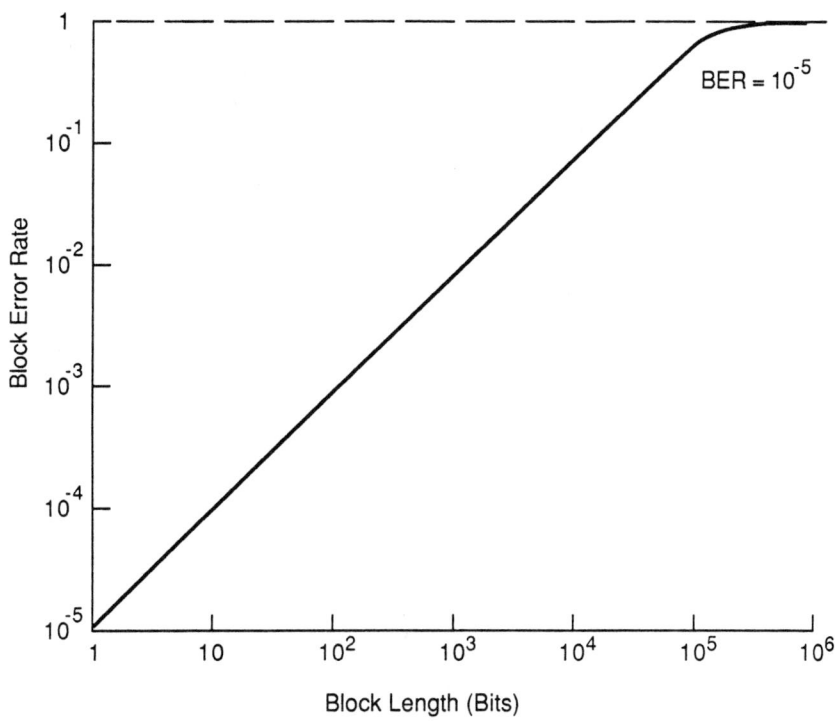

Figure 5.4
Block Error Rate vs Block Length

5.6 SELECTING A TRANSMISSION MEDIUM

I have presented many concepts related to the transmission characteristics of a raw transmission medium or, in my terminology, the transmission-level performance characterization of a transmission medium. In this section, I apply some of the concepts developed here to guide a system designer's choice when faced with the problem of selecting a transmission medium for a computer communication network.

5.6.1 Case Study 1

A transmission system can transport n_1 messages of class 1, or n_2 messages of class 2, or n_3 messages of class 3, or n_n messages of class n, per unit time. Each message of a particular class has the same number of bits (i.e., l_1 bits per message for class 1, l_2 bits per message for class 2, etc).

If the transmission system is required to carry a mixture of the different classes of messages, with message class i occurring with probability p_i, derive an expression giving the total number of messages carried by the transmission system per unit time on the average.

Solution: From the data given, it follows that the channel capacity of the system can be expressed as:

$$C = n_1 l_1 = n_2 l_2 = \ldots = n_n l_n \text{ bits/second} \quad (5.19)$$

Let N messages be carried by the system per unit time. Then, the system transmits $p_1 N$ messages of class 1, $p_2 N$ messages of class 2, and so on. Therefore the system channel capacity can also be expressed as;

$$C = \sum_{i=1}^{n} p_i N l_i \quad (5.20)$$

From Equations (5.19) and (5.20),

$$\sum_{i=1}^{n} p_i N l_i = n_i l_i$$

or

$$N = \frac{n_i l_i}{\sum_{i=1}^{n} p_i l_i}$$

or

$$\frac{1}{N} = \frac{p_1 l_1 + p_2 l_2 + \cdots + p_n l_n}{n_i l_i}$$

Selecting a Transmission Medium

$$= \frac{p_1}{n_1} + \frac{p_2}{n_2} + \cdots + \frac{p_n}{n_n}$$

Stated in words, I have shown that the number of messages carried is the weighted harmonic mean of the number of messages from each class.

5.6.2 Case Study 2

Two data transmission systems, A and B, have the following transmission characteristics:

System	Error Rate	Transmission Efficiency bits/second/Hz
A	p_1	a_1
B	p_2	a_2

Given

$$0 \leq p_1, p_2 \leq 1$$

and

$$a_1, a_2 > 0$$

and assuming that

(1) the cost of transmission is proportional to the bandwidth

(2) for every bit correctly received, your client generates one unit of revenue

(3) for every bit incorrectly received, your client has to pay back 10 units of revenue to his or her customer

which system would you recommend as a system designer to your client?

Solution: Since the cost of transmission is proportional to the bandwidth for both systems, let the client buy unit bandwidth for either system for the same price.

For System 1 we have:

number of bits transmitted correctly $= (1 - p_1)a_1$

number of bits transmitted in error $= p_1 a_1$

Therefore, revenue generated by System 1 $= (1 - p_1)a_1 - 10 p_1 a_1$

$$= a_1 - 11 p_1 a_1$$

Similarly, revenue generated by System 2 $= (1 - p_2) a_2 - 10 p_2 a_2$

$$= a_2 - 11 p_2 a_2$$

System 1 is preferable to System 2 if

$$a_1 - 11 p_1 a_1 > a_2 - 11 p_2 a_2$$

or if

$$\frac{a_1}{a_2} > \frac{1 - 11 p_2}{1 - 11 p_1} \tag{5.21}$$

which is the required result.

5.7 REFERENCES

[1] D. J. Horton and P. G. Bowie, "An Overview of Dataroute: System and Performance" <u>Proc. Int. Conf. on Comm.</u>, Minneapolis, June 1974, pp. 2A1-2A5.

[2] J. J. Mahoney, Jr., J. J. Mansell, and R. C. Matlack, "User's View of the Network," <u>Bell System Technical Journal</u>, Vol. 54, No. 5, May 1975, pp. 833-844.

[3] P. K. Verma, S. G. S. Shiva, N. D. Georganas, and J. S. Jawanda, "Evaluation of the Mean Error-Free Interval of a Noisy Data Channel," <u>IEEE Trans. on Comm.</u>, Vol. Com-26, No. 1, January 1978, pp. 185-187.

Chapter 6

COMMUNICATION-LEVEL PERFORMANCE

This chapter introduces the concept of error correction in the transmission process in order to insure that the residual error performance or the user perceived error performance is better than the error performance of the raw transmission medium. Two techniques of error correction — forward and backward — are examined. The trade-off between a better error environment and additional delay or lower throughput is studied.

6.1 SENSITIVITIES OF APPLICATIONS TO THE ERROR ENVIRONMENT

I have discussed performance at the transmission level in Chapter 5. The transmission-level performance is governed by characteristics of the transmission medium, for example, its error performance. Characteristics of a particular medium of transmission are relatively invariant. For example, free space and the atmosphere, which constitute the transmission medium for satellite communication, have transmission characteristics that are not amenable to change. The transmission characteristics of a coaxial cable are similarly defined by its geometry. Optical fibers are characterized by the refractive indices of the inner and the outer sheaths, their diameters, and their transparencies.

We have also seen previously that the end-to-end error performance requirement for data is a function of the specific application. Loss or mutilation of a single digit could be disastrous in a financial transaction. On the other hand, text transmission can usually tolerate character errors due to the high redundancy inherent in natural languages.

It would be impractical to have different transmission media for different applications even though the error performance requirements of the different applications might differ substantially. Fortunately, several error correction techniques are available which ensure that, for applications where it is required, the residual error (i.e., the error remaining after correction) is lower than the error performance which characterizes the raw transmission medium. If no error correction techniques were employed, the resultant error performance would be the same as the error performance of the raw transmission medium and, therefore, unacceptable for an application demanding a higher level of error performance. Using techniques of error correction, it is entirely possible that different portions of the aggregate speed of the same physical transmission medium have different residual error environments. For example, a T1 line which is carrying both voice and data in its different 64 kbps channels can have its voice channels provide adequate performance without the use of any error correction techniques. On the other hand, the data channels may be providing a substantially better error performance through the use of an error correction technique on an end-to-end basis.

6.2 TECHNIQUES FOR ERROR CORRECTION

There are two basic techniques of error correction: (1) Forward Error Correction, and (2) Backward Error Correction. In forward error correction, appropriate redundant bits are introduced along with the user data bits in such a way that the functions of detecting an error and subsequently correcting it are both accomplished using the redundant bits transmitted along with the user data.

The backward error correction technique, on the other hand, uses a technique to code the data in such a way that the receiver can only detect errors in the received data (without correcting them), using a relatively small amount of overhead bits transmitted along with the user data bits. Once an error is detected, the receiver, using a reverse communication channel, requests a retransmission of the corrupted data.

6.3 FORWARD ERROR CORRECTION

Forward error correction techniques have been commercially employed over at least the past fifty years. They are especially suited to situations where bits in error are relatively independent and it is impractical or difficult to have a reverse channel for communicating the receipt of bad data by the receiver to the sending entity. The devising of good and practical error correcting codes is an extensive field of mathematics by itself. Here, we will simply show that error correction is possible under most situations by the use of a technique that transmits check digits in addition to message digits or user data [1].

Forward Error Correction

Assume that the user data is organized into sequences of 16 successive bits followed by a sequence of 8 check bits that are derived as shown by the following example. Let the user data be 1101 0011 0101 1001. In order to find the appropriate check bits, we write the user data in a 4 by 4 grid as:

1	1	0	1
0	0	1	1
0	1	0	1
1	0	0	1

Next, we associate with each row and each column a bit that is derived such that there is an even number of 1s in each row and each column. The new grid will now appear as:

	0	0	1	0
1	1	1	0	1
0	0	0	1	1
0	0	1	0	1
0	1	0	0	1

It can be easily seen that the check bits introduced make the number of 1s in each row and column an even number. The check bits are then transmitted along with the user data bits to the receiving end.

If one of the sixteen single bits of user data is corrupted in the process of transmission, one single row and one single column of the 4 by 4 user data grid will show violation of the parity. The grid point at which the row and the column showing this violation intersect identifies the bit in error. It follows that as long as the number of bits in error in the 16 bits of user data is limited to 1, the method provides a foolproof means of error correction.

Should a single error be made in the transmission of one of the check bits, there will be an odd number of 1s in some row *or* in some column (but not in both as was the case when one of the user data bits was in error). In this case, we know that one of the check bits is in error and the user data bits are correct. We merely discard the check bits and recover the transmitted user data bits. Again, as long as the number of check bits in error is no more than one, it will be corrected.

The error correcting code discussed above is called the row-column sum parity check code. We have seen that this code corrects all single errors. If there are double errors, it can either incorrectly correct the user data bits or detect such errors but not uniquely correct them. In the latter case, it may be acceptable in certain situations to merely discard the received data. In situations, where it might be possible to request a retransmission of the user data, one would do so.

The example discussed above uses 8 check bits for a total of 16 user data bits. This gives the code a bandwidth requirement which is 50% higher than that required if there were no check bits. One could, of course, increase the size of the grid and thus reduce the number of check bits relative to the number of user data bits. For example, a 24 by 24 user data grid will have 576 user data bits and only 48 check bits, increasing the bandwidth requirement by a mere 8.33%. However, with a larger number of bits, the probability of having two or more bits in error will correspondingly increase, reducing the effectiveness with which the code corrects the error.

It is clear that the price one pays in eliminating, or more exactly, reducing, transmission errors using a forward error correcting technique is by way of transmitting redundant bits along with actual data bits. If the channel speed were kept constant, the transmission time would increase. On the other hand, if the transmission time were to remain constant, a higher-speed line would be necessary. In either case, the price is easily computed. The increase in transmission time would be by a factor of the total number of bits (i.e., user data bits plus redundant bits) to the number of user data bits. The efficacy of a forward error correcting code would be thus determined by these two factors, namely, the robustness of the code in correcting errors on one hand and the expense of overhead bits on the other.

6.4 BACKWARD ERROR CORRECTION

As indicated earlier, the backward error correction technique accomplishes correction through the process of retransmission. It is especially suitable for block transmission of data where bits in error are highly correlated. This characteristic is typical of most transmission systems. Relatively robust codes, known as cyclic codes, have been devised that can detect a wide variety of errors, reducing the residual error rate to as low as 10^{-12} or 10^{-13} from transmission facilities characterized by error rates of 10^{-6} or even higher. The overhead of coding bits is relatively low and in the range of 10-15%.

The backward error correction technique provides a powerful means of error correction in most situations and is, therefore, widely used. Before we take a look at the technique of cyclic coding, we will first study its implications.

6.5 IMPLICATIONS OF CYCLIC CODING

Let there be n bits per block of user data to be transmitted. Let s be the channel speed in bits per second, so that the transmission time of a block of user data is n/s seconds. The cyclic redundancy code will add, say, r bits to each block, thus increasing the transmission time to $(n + r)/s$ seconds.

Implications of Cyclic Coding

Let the transmission medium be characterized by a bit error rate of p. For simplicity, we assume that bits in error are randomly distributed. The probability that any designated single bit is correctly received is $(1-p)$. This gives the probability of correct reception of all the bits in the block, including the overhead bits, as $(1-p)^{n+r}$. Therefore, the probability P that at least one of the bits is in error is given by,

$$P = 1 - (1-p)^{n+r} \tag{6.1}$$

Obviously, P is the probability that a block will have to be retransmitted.

In order to compute the implications of cyclic coding on the throughput and delay, we further assume that the transmission medium provides a propagation delay of d seconds in either direction. Further, for simplicity, we assume that the detection of error takes a negligible amount of time. (This is usually the case when the computations related to checking the accuracy of the received block are carried out in hardware or firmware.) In addition, we assume that the transmission time associated with a negative acknowledgement is also negligible and that the requested retransmission begins without a significant delay after the request for retransmission is received.

There is no guarantee that a block that was retransmitted after one or more errors are detected in it will arrive correctly on the second attempt. Indeed, a block may be subject to several retransmissions, each with exponentially reducing probabilities of error.

Using the parameters we have defined earlier, we can now construct the following table:

(1) No transmission error:

$$\text{Probability} = 1 - P$$

$$\text{Number of user data bits} = n$$

$$\text{Total number of bits transmitted} = n + r$$

$$\text{Total delay} = \frac{n+r}{s} + d$$

$$\text{Relative throughput} = \frac{n}{n+r}$$

(2) Correct reception after one retransmission:

$$\text{Probability} = P(1-P)$$

$$\text{Number of user data bits} = n$$

$$\text{Total number of bits transmitted} = 2(n+r)$$

$$\text{Total delay} = \frac{2(n+r)}{s} + 3d$$

$$\text{Relative throughput} = \frac{n}{2(n+r)}$$

(3) Correct reception after two retransmissions:

$$\text{Probability} = P^2(1-p)$$

$$\text{Number of user data bits} = n$$

$$\text{Total number of bits transmitted} = 3(n+r)$$

$$\text{Total delay} = \frac{3(n+r)}{s} + 5d$$

$$\text{Relative throughput} = \frac{n}{3(n+r)}$$

The sequence can be generalized so that for correct reception after m retransmissions, we have,

$$\text{Probability} = P^m(1-P)$$

$$\text{Number of user data bits} = n$$

$$\text{Total number of bits transmitted} = (m+1)(n+r)$$

$$\text{Total delay} = \frac{(m+1)(n+r)}{s} + (2m+1)d$$

$$\text{Relative throughput} = \frac{n}{(m+1)(n+r)}$$

The mean time taken to send a block can thus be given by the sum of the delays weighted by their probabilities, that is,

$$\text{Mean delay} = \sum_{m=0}^{\infty} P^m(1-P) \left[\frac{(m+1)(n+r)}{s} + (2m+1)d \right]$$

$$= \frac{(1-P)}{s} \sum_{m=0}^{\infty} P^m \left[m(n+r+2sd) + (n+r+sd) \right]$$

$$= \frac{1-P}{s} \left[\sum_{m=0}^{\infty} P^m \left[m(n+r+2sd) \right] + \sum_{m=0}^{\infty} P^m(n+r+sd) \right]$$

$$= \frac{1-P}{s} \left[(n+r+2sd) \sum_{m=0}^{\infty} P^m \cdot m + \frac{n+r+sd}{1-P} \right]$$

$$= \frac{1-P}{s} \left[(n+r+2sd)(P + 2P^2 + 3P^3 + \ldots) + \frac{n+r+sd}{1-P} \right]$$

$$= \frac{1-P}{s} \left[P(n+r+2sd)(1 + 2P + 3P^2 + \ldots) + \frac{n+r+sd}{1-P} \right]$$

$$= \frac{1-P}{s} \left[P(n+r+2sd) \frac{1}{(1-P)^2} + \frac{n+r+sd}{1-P} \right]$$

$$= \frac{P(n+r+2sd)}{s(1-P)} + \frac{n+r+sd}{s}$$

$$= \frac{n+r+sd(1+P)}{s(1-P)} \tag{6.3}$$

after some algebraic manipulations

Recall that in the absence of the error correction procedure employed here, the total delay incurred in sending a block of user data bits is

$$\frac{n}{s} + d$$

or

$$\frac{n+sd}{s} \tag{6.4}$$

It can easily be seen that the numerator of Equation (6.3) is always greater than that of Equation (6.4). On the other hand, the opposite is true for their respective denominators. It then follows that Equation (6.3) is always numerically greater than Equation (6.4). Their ratio, the relative delay, is given by:

$$\text{Relative delay} = \frac{n + r + sd(1 + P)}{(n + sd)(1 - P)} \qquad (6.5)$$

It can be seen that the relative delay is always greater than 1; the asymptotic value of 1 is reached when there are no overhead bits, that is, $r = 0$ and the block error rate P approaches zero. The relative throughput can similarly be computed as:

$$\begin{aligned}
\text{Relative throughput} &= \sum_{m=0}^{\infty} P^m(1 - P) \frac{n}{(m + 1)(n + r)} \\
&= \frac{n(1 - P)}{n + r} \sum_{m=0}^{\infty} \frac{P^m}{m + 1} \\
&= \frac{n(1 - P)}{n + r} \left[1 + \frac{P}{2} + \frac{P^2}{3} + \frac{P^3}{4} + \cdots \right] \\
&= \frac{n(1 - P)}{(n + r)P} \left[P + \frac{P^2}{2} + \frac{P^3}{3} + \frac{P^4}{4} + \cdots \right] \\
&= \frac{n(1 - P)}{(n + r)P} \int_0^P (1 + P + P^2 + \cdots)\, dp \\
&= \frac{n(1 - P)}{(n + r)P} \int_0^P \frac{dP}{1 - P} \\
&= \frac{n(1 - P)}{(n + r)P} \ln \frac{1}{1 - P} \qquad (6.6)
\end{aligned}$$

It can be shown that the relative throughput is always smaller than unity. Its value reaches 1 asymptotically when there are no overhead bits, that is, $r = 0$, and the block error rate P approaches zero.

6.6 THE EFFECT OF PROPAGATION DELAY

With finite values of propagation delay, it is obvious that the transmission channel will become idle for a period of time if a frame-by-frame acknowledgment was mandated by the protocol used, that is, if the protocol used required that before a new frame is sent by the sending entity, the correct receipt of the last frame must have been acknowledged.

Idle time on the channel reduces throughput. Therefore, most practical protocols in use today allow up to a certain number of frames w — also known as the window — to be outstanding before stopping transmission. For example, if the value of w is eight, up to eight consecutive frames can be outstanding. The minimum value of the window for continuous transmission is obviously related to the propagation delay, the transmission line speed and the frame size.

In order to derive a relationship between the related variables, let

n = number of bits per frame

s = channel speed (bits/second)

d = propagation delay (seconds)

w = window size

The transmission time required to send a frame is n/s. Because of the propagation delay associated with the channel, it will take an additional d seconds before the frame is received. The receiver will take an additional time t_r to check the received frame and generate the acknowledgement signal which will arrive at the transmitting end d seconds later (assuming that the acknowledgment signal itself is sufficiently short).

The total delay associated with the receipt of an acknowledgement is, therefore,

$$n/s + 2d + t_r \qquad (6.7)$$

In order for data transfer to take place continuously, this time must be less than or equal to the transmission time associated with sending w frames, that is,

$$n/s + 2d + t_r \leq w\, n/s \qquad (6.8)$$

6.7 CYCLIC REDUNDANCY CODING (CRC)

In order to understand the technique of cyclic redundancy coding, assume that the data block to be transmitted consists of n bits. This can be represented by a polynomial of degree $(n - 1)$ having up to n terms. For example if the data block is 1101101, its polynomial representation is:

$$x^6 + x^5 + x^3 + x^2 + 1$$

in terms of an arbitrary variable x. The assumption here is that the digit farthest to the left in the message carries the highest weight; in this case it is in the 2^6 position. The polynomial is written from left to right with powers of x in descending order and its coefficients being the corresponding binary digit (i.e., 1 or 0) sequentially.

All algebraic manipulations on the polynomial are performed using addition and multiplication under modulo-2 arithmetic rules. The rules of modulo-2 arithmetic are (see also Section 3.1.5):

$$0 + 0 = 0, \quad 1 + 0 = 1, \quad 0 + 1 = 1, \text{ and } 1 + 1 = 0$$

Using these rules, we have, for example,

$$(x^6 + x^4 + x^2 + x + 1) + (x^5 + x^2 + 1)$$
$$= x^6 + x^5 + x^4 + x$$

Multiplications of the same expressions can be written as:

$$(x^6 + x^4 + x^2 + x + 1)(x^5 + x^2 + 1)$$
$$= x^{11} + x^8 + x^6 + x^9 + x^6 + x^4 + x^7 + x^4$$
$$+ x^2 + x^6 + x^3 + x + x^5 + x^2 + 1$$
$$= x^{11} + x^9 + x^8 + x^7 + x^6 + x^5 + x^3 + x + 1$$

A division of the two polynomials can, similarly, be shown to be expressed as follows:

$$\frac{x^6 + x^4 + x^2 + x + 1}{x^5 + x^2 + 1} = x + \frac{x^4 + x^3 + x^2 + 1}{x^5 + x^2 + 1}$$

Let the user data written in a polynomial form be called $m(x)$. In general $m(x)$ can be expressed as:

$$m(x) = q_n x^n + q_{n-1} x^{n-1} + \ldots + q_1 x + q_0$$

Cyclic Redundancy Coding (CRC)

The coefficients $q's$ can have a value 0 or 1 depending upon whether the user data bit in the particular position has the value 0 or 1. To transmit the user data block, we need a second polynomial $g(x)$ of degree r. The polynomial to be actually transmitted on the line $t(x)$ is obtained as discussed below. We first perform the following algebraic operation in modulo-2 arithmetic:

$$\frac{x^r m(x)}{g(x)} = Q(x) + \frac{r(x)}{g(x)} \quad (6.9)$$

$$t(x) = x^r\, m(x) + r(x) \quad (6.10)$$

Obviously, the polynomial to be transmitted $t(x)$ is of degree $(n + r)$, and the total number of bits to be transmitted is $(n + r + 1)$ instead of $(n + 1)$ if no CRC is to be used. The technique therefore reduces throughput by a factor $(n + 1)/(n + r + 1)$.

From (6.9) we have,

$$x^r\, m(x) = Q(x)g(x) + r(x) \quad (6.11)$$

Substituting for $x^r\, m(x)$ in (6.10), we get

$$t(x) = Q(x)g(x) \quad (6.12)$$

It follows from (6.12), that the polynomial to be transmitted $t(x)$ is fully divisible by the generator polynomial $g(x)$. Since $g(x)$ is predetermined and known at the receiving end, we use this property of exact divisibility to determine if the transmitted data was corrupted in the transmission process. In other words, if the received polynomial is not exactly divisible by $g(x)$, it is discarded and a retransmission requested.

As an example, let the user data block be, as before, 1101101, such that

$$m(x) = x^6 + x^5 + x^3 + x^2 + 1$$

Choose the generator polynomial, $g(x)$, as

$$g(x) = x^3 + x + 1$$

The degree r of the generator polynomial is 3, so that

$$x^r\, m(x) = x^9 + x^8 + x^6 + x^5 + x^3$$

The polynomial division $\dfrac{x^r m(x)}{g(x)}$ is now performed as follows:

$$
\begin{array}{r}
x^6 + x^5 + x^4 + x^3 + x^2 + x^1 \\
x^3 + x + 1 \,\overline{\big)\, x^9 + x^8 + x^6 + x^5 + x^3 } \\
\underline{x^9 + x^7 + x^6 } \\
x^8 + x^7 + x^5 + x^3 \\
\underline{x^8 + x^6 + x^5 } \\
x^7 + x^6 + x^3 \\
\underline{x^7 + x^5 + x^4 } \\
x^6 + x^5 + x^4 + x^3 \\
\underline{x^6 + x^4 + x^3 } \\
x^5 \\
\underline{x^5 + x^3 + x^2 } \\
x^3 + x^2 \\
\underline{x^3 + x + 1} \\
x^2 + x + 1
\end{array}
$$

The message to be transmitted, $t(x)$, is now

$$t(x) = x^3(x^6 + x^5 + x^3 + x^2 + 1) + x^2 + x + 1$$

$$= x^9 + x^8 + x^6 + x^5 + x^3 + x^2 + x + 1$$

which is equivalent to

$$1101101111$$

Since the CRC technique uses the property of exact divisibility it follows that if the received polynomial is corrupted by error but the error pattern is such that the resulting polynomial is still divisible by $g(x)$, the error will go undetected and, therefore, uncorrected.

6.8 DEGREE OF PROTECTION FROM ERROR PROVIDED BY THE CYCLIC REDUNDANCY CODE

Generally speaking, the forward error correction technique involves a substantial overhead for error correction. In addition, it is usually less effective in situations where bits in error are correlated. As it happens, for most communication systems used for data transmission, bits in error are highly correlated; it is usual to see clean transmission of data with bunches of bits in error occurring together. For this reason, the technique of forward error correction is seldom used in commercial transmission systems. Most error correction techniques in use today are based on transmission of data in blocks, each block appended by a CRC code word derived as explained in the previous section.

The choice of the generating polynomial is made such that the probability of undetected errors is minimized. In order to understand the effectiveness of the CRC coding, assume that the transmitted polynomial $t(x)$ is received as a polynomial $t'(x)$ corrupted by noise, where

$$t'(x) = t(x) + e(x)$$

$e(x)$ representing the polynomial of bits in error.

It follows that if $e(x)$ is exactly divisible by $g(x)$, no error will be detected. If, however, $e(x)$ is not exactly divisible by $g(x)$, the received sequence of bits in the frame will be declared by the receiver to contain one or more bits in error. A request for retransmission will be made and the received data will be discarded.

Single bit errors will be represented by the polynomial

$$e(x) = x^i \quad i \leq n + r$$

If the generator polynomial has more than one term, $e(x)$ will not be exactly divisible by $g(x)$. This will result in all single-bit errors being detected by the CRC coding. Extending the same argument, it follows that all 2-bit errors will also be detected if the generator polynomial has at least three terms. Further extending this argument, it follows that all bursts of errors where the number of bits in that burst are less than or equal to the degree of the generating polynomial will be detected. In other words, for a generating polynomial of degree r, all error bursts of length less than $r + 1$ bits will be detected.

For an error burst of exactly $r + 1$ bits in length, since the first and the last bits in the burst are in error by definition, it follows that the remaining $r - 1$ bits must be identical to the bits of the generating polynomial. Assuming the error environment to be random, the probability of this happening is

$$\left[\frac{1}{2}\right]^{r-1} \qquad (6.13)$$

If $r = 16$ as in expression (6.13), an error burst of length equal to exactly 17 bits will go undetected with a probability

$$\left[\frac{1}{2}\right]^{15} \text{ or } .00003$$

Considering that the probability of occurrence of a 17-bit error pattern is itself low, the CRC provides a very high degree of protection.

Should the generator polynomial have $(x + 1)$ as one of its factors, it will detect all odd numbers of errors. This can be proved as follows:

Let $e(x)$ have an odd number of terms. For the error to go undetected, $e(x)$ must be exactly divisible by $(x + 1)$, that is,

$$e(x) = (x + 1) f(x)$$

This will imply

$$e(1) = (1 + 1) f(x) = 0$$

which is contrary to the assumption since, if $e(x)$ contained an odd number of terms, $e(1)$ will not be equal to zero in modulo-2 arithmetic.

The degree of protection provided by the cyclic redundancy code is sufficient for almost all applications. As the degree of the generating polynomial is increased, the protection against undetected errors increases. The International Standards Organization (ISO) has proposed the following generating polynomial for applying the Cyclic Redundancy Check:

$$x^{16} + x^{12} + x^5 + 1 \qquad (6.14)$$

It can be shown that the probability of failing to detect errors by the use of a CRC polynomial such as in Equation (6.14) is very low, several orders of magnitude lower than the error rate of the raw transmission medium for data blocks of commonly used sizes. Actual measurements on data have been shown to be reasonably close to the theoretical prediction [2].

6.9 DELAY, THROUGHPUT, AND THE ERROR ENVIRONMENT

We have seen in this chapter that the transmission error environment can be improved considerably at the expense of additional delay and lower throughput. It turns out that this trade-off gives the necessary protection without introducing intolerable delays or unacceptable inefficiencies of channel usage. The precise advantage gained and the associated costs by way of higher delays and lower throughput can be computed as shown in this chapter. It should be remembered that the error protection provided by using any of the mechanisms discussed here also requires additional electronic circuitry with attendant costs as well as reliability factors associated with the use of additional hardware and software.

6.10 REFERENCES

[1] J. R. Pierce and E. C. Posner, *Introduction to Communication Science and Systems*, Plenum Press, New York, 1980.

[2] J. Martin, Teleprocessing Network Organization, Prentice-Hall, Inc., Englewood Cliffs, N.J., 1961, Chapter 5.

Chapter 7

CUSTOMER PERCEIVED DELAYS IN A PACKET SWITCHED NETWORK*

This chapter prescribes a methodology to estimate the customer perceived or end-to-end delays in a packet switched network. The major elements that determine the end-to-end performance are specified and, in particular, the influence of the maximum packet size permissible in the network is assessed. The end-to-end delay analysis is carried out separately for character-at-a-time terminals and block oriented terminals. The chapter also presents a general procedure for estimating percentile response times when response time is composed of a number of components, some of which are continuously distributed and the remaining discretely distributed. This situation is common in the evaluation of percentile response times in a packet switched network.

7.1 END-TO-END DELAYS

7.1.1 Importance of End-to-End Delays

The major elements that determine customer perceived or end-to-end performance stem from the constraints imposed by the user and his application, the access media and the common-user-network performance.

---

* Portions of this chapter are reprinted, with permission, from Proc. National Telecommunications Conf., Houston, November-December, 1980, pp. 25.1.1-25.1.5 (© IEEE 1980), and from Proc. Int. Conf. on Comm., Seattle, June 1980, pp. 61.5.1-61.5.4 (© IEEE 1980).

Delay analyses for computer communication networks can be viewed from the perspectives of the network itself or from an end-to-end perspective. The latter will include the components of delay that are attributable to the access subsystems under the specific user's application environment. This chapter analyzes the mean end-to-end delay perceived by the user with an inquiry-response application using a single terminal per line access configuration and a packet switched common user network while interacting with a remote computer. Both character-at-a-time and block oriented terminals are considered. The mean end-to-end delay, hereafter referred to as the Mean Response Time (MRT), is defined as the mean time from the transmission of the last character of an inquiry to the receipt of the first character of the response.

For many interactive applications, a knowledge of MRT is not usually sufficient. This chapter also discusses a procedure for estimating the end-to-end percentile response times.

Delay in packet switched networks has been the subject of extensive studies [1,2,3,4,5]. Most such studies have focused on the queuing and processing delays that a packet suffers while transiting a node. The network itself can be viewed as a collection of nodes interconnected by transmission facilities. The delay the network provides (i.e., the end-to-end delay excluding the components of delay attributable to the access subsystems) is, therefore, the sum of delays suffered by the packet at the network nodes and those in the interconnecting transmission facilities.

In this book, we look at the packet switched network as an integral whole typified by a variable delay [6]. It is important to keep this perspective when we focus on the end-to-end delay. From our perspective, then, the end-to-end delay is composed of the delay attributable to the network and that attributable to the access subsystems.

7.1.2 End-to-End Delays in Packet Switched Networks

A recent study [7] conducted for the Hartford Graduate Center reports on the delay and throughput characteristics of several packet switched networks. Figure 7.1 shows a schematic diagram of the arrangement used. Four packet switched networks — Telenet, Tymnet, Uninet and Conn-net — were studied. The packet switched networks were connected to the host via a 9.6 kbits/sec line using the X.25 protocol. In addition, remote access through wide-area telephone service (WATS) and modems terminating on a Micom X.25 packet assembler disassembler was also used. All communications circuits terminated in an IBM 3705 front-end processor.

The experiment measured the short- and long-packet response times. The time between transmitting the last character of the command and receiving the single character response is the response time for the short, one-character packet. For measuring the long-packet response time, the experiment entered

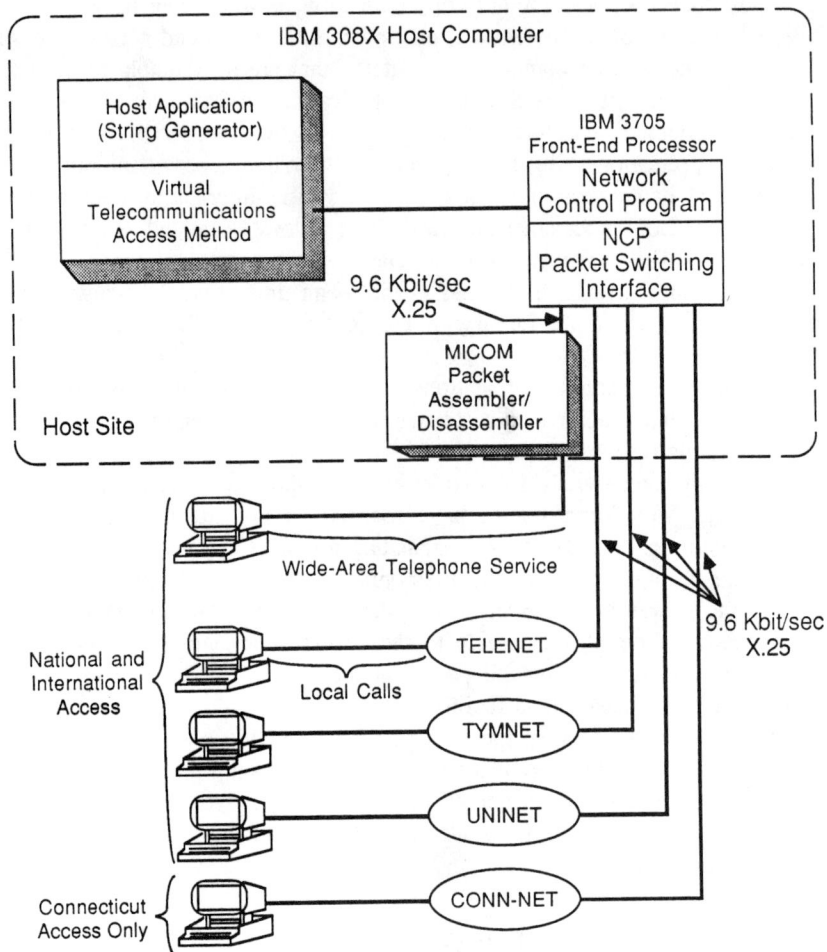

Figure 7.1
Comparative Measurements on Packet Switched Networks*

a command requesting the transmission of 2000 characters from the host. The time between the transmitting of the last character of the command and the first character of the response is the long-packet response time.

Tables 7.1 and 7.2 present the statistics of the short-packet and the long-packet response times for the different networks.

---

* Reprinted from January 1987 <u>Data Communications</u>. Copyright 1/87 McGraw-Hill, Inc. All rights reserved.

Table 7.1
Short-packet response time (in seconds)*

Vendor	Sample	Mean	Standard Deviation	Minimum	Maximum
Micom	3713	0.33	0.06	0.21	0.71
Conn-net	3247	0.41	0.06	0.32	0.82
Uninet	2328	0.71	0.20	0.44	5.38
Telenet	1753	0.73	0.21	0.44	3.57
Tymnet	2327	1.13	0.46	0.49	8.52

* Reprinted from January 1987 Data Communications. Copyright 1/87; McGraw-Hill, Inc. All rights reserved.

Table 7.2
Long-packet response time (in seconds)*

Vendor	Sample	Mean	Standard Deviation	Minimum	Maximum
Micom	361	0.46	0.05	0.38	0.72
Conn-net	323	0.57	0.05	0.44	0.77
Uninet	222	1.05	0.18	0.70	1.76
Telenet	167	1.13	0.24	0.76	1.80
Tymnet	216	1.50	0.62	0.65	5.61

* Reprinted from January 1987 Data Communications, Copyright 1/87, McGraw-Hill, Inc. All rights reserved.

7.2 THE CHARACTER-AT-A-TIME TERMINAL

7.2.1 Elements of End-to-End Delays

Figure 7.2 depicts a character-at-a-time terminal communicating with a remote computer over a packet switched network. The access line speeds at the terminal and the host end are s_1 and s_2 respectively. The terminal user is capable of entering information at a (maximum) rate of s ($<s_1$). The information from the computer is entered into the network at the line rate s_2.

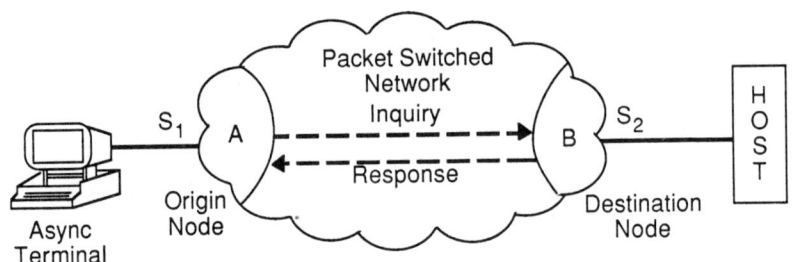

MRT Components

1. Transit delay A to B = T_1
2. Interference delay at B = T_2
3. Last packet transmission delay (inquiry) at B = T_3
4. Host delay = T_4
5. First packet transmission delay (response) at B = T_5
6. Transit delay (response) B to A = T_6

Figure 7.2
Delay Components of the Character-at-a-Time Terminal*

---

* P. K. Verma, "Customer Perceived Delays in a Packet Switched Network," <u>Proc. National Telecommunications Conf.,</u> Houston, November-December, 1980, pp. 25.1.1-25.1.5 © IEEE 1980.

Should an inquiry message exceed in length the maximum packet size (N), the first full packet will be dispatched to the remote end as soon as the first N characters have been received by the network. The same will be the case for each subsequent packet until the last packet, which will depart immediately after the last character has been entered. Single packet inquiry messages will be dispatched immediately after the entry of the last character. A similar discipline will apply at the host end.

Using the definition of MRT given in Section 7.1, it follows that the user does not perceive any delay due to the packetization process at the network node interfacing his or her terminal.* The assessment of MRT is carried out by subdividing the end-to-end delay into six different components, T_1 through T_6.

The network itself is modeled as providing a mean transit delay, T_1, to each packet. Specifically, T_1 is defined as the mean time between the receipt by the network of the last character of a packet and the time the first character is ready to depart from the network to the destination computer or terminal. Note that, in general, T_1 is a function of the packet length.

Using the above definition of T_1, the last packet of an inquiry will arrive at the destination node after a (mean) time T_1 and will be buffered by the destination node.** Should the previous packet, if any, have departed in full, the last packet will not be required to wait and its transmission to the host will be initiated at once. On the other hand, if the previous packet has not departed in full, the last packet must wait until it has. This waiting period, termed the interference delay, will be represented by T_2. T_3 will represent the last packet transmission delay to the host and will obviously depend upon the mean size of the last packet and the host access line speed.

The fourth component of the MRT, T_4, is the delay within the host from the time the inquiry has been received in full to the time the entire response is available for transfer to the network.

The response from the host will be blocked and packetized at the host node before being forwarded to the inquiring terminal. This (mean) packetization delay is referred to as T_5. Since the MRT involves a delay up to the receipt of the first character of the response,† the statistics of the first packet (of the

---

* Delay equivalent to a character at the access line speed to transport the last character of the inquiry to the network has been neglected.

** The difference between the times of arrival of the first and the last characters of a packet in transiting from one network node to another is considered negligible. This assumption is justified since the internal network trunk speeds are usually at least an order of magnitude higher than the access line speeds. The mean transit delay is thus assumed to be independent of packet size.

† The one character delay involved in receiving the first character has been neglected.

response) will determine T_5. T_6 is the transit delay applicable to the first response packet and is the same as T_1, transit delay for the last inquiry packet. If the variables network transit delay (mean value = T_1) and host delay (mean value = T_4) are mutually independent and are also independent of the user's demands, an arithmetic sum of the means of the six variables $\sum_{i=1}^{6} T_i$ will yield the MRT. This is the approach we adopt here [6].

7.2.2 Evaluation of Delay Components

The Mean Network Transit Delay T_1 (or T_6) is a performance characteristic of the network. Typical values of T_1 range in hundreds of milliseconds. For the numerical example worked out in Section 4, a value of 500 milliseconds for T_1 has been assumed.

The interference delay (mean value = T_2) defined earlier will arise when the time to forward the last packet (i.e., the time interval between the reception of the first and the last characters of the last packet) by the originating node is smaller than the time to transmit the second to last packet from the destination node to the host. If we assume that s is the speed at which characters are being generated by the user's terminal ($s \leq s_1$) and k (a variable) is the length of the last packet, then interference delay will arise whenever*

$$\frac{N}{s_2} > \frac{k}{s} \qquad (7.1)$$

It also follows that the magnitude of this delay is given by

$$\frac{N}{s_2} - \frac{k}{s} \qquad (7.2)$$

The mean value of Equation (7.2) will yield the Mean Interference Delay T_2. If we assume $P(k)$ to be the probability distribution function associated with the last packet, we have:

---

* An implicit assumption here is that any variation in the value of T_1 encountered by adjacent packets is small.

$$T_2 = \sum_{k=1}^{M} P(k) \left\{ \frac{N}{s_2} - \frac{k}{s} \right\} \qquad (7.3)$$

where M is the nearest integer equal to or lower than sN/s_2.

Assuming the inquiry messages to be geometrically distributed with a mean of $1/\mu_i$, $P(k)$ has been evaluated (Appendix 7A) as:

$$P(k) = \frac{\mu_i}{1 - (1 - \mu_i)^N} (1 - \mu_i)^{k-1}, \quad k = 1, 2, \ldots, N \qquad (7.4)$$

Using Equation (7.4) in Equation (7.3), we obtain

$$T_2 = \frac{\mu_i}{1 - (1 - \mu_i)^N} \sum_{k=1}^{M} (1 - \mu_i)^{k-1} \left\{ \frac{N}{s_2} - \frac{k}{s} \right\}$$

$$= \frac{\mu_i}{1 - (1 - \mu_i)^N} \left\{ \frac{N}{s_2} \frac{1 - (1 - \mu_i)^M}{\mu_i} \right.$$

$$\left. - \frac{1}{s} \frac{1 - (M+1)(1 - \mu_i)^M + M(1 - \mu_i)^{M+1}}{\mu_i^2} \right\} \qquad (7.5)$$

The delay component T_3 represents the last inquiry packet transmission delay (from the network to the host). T_3 can be evaluated from Equation (7A4) and the host access line speed s_2. We have

$$T_3 = \frac{1 - (N+1)(1 - \mu_i)^N + N(1 - \mu_i)^{N+1}}{s_2 \mu_i \{1 - (1 - \mu_i)^N\}} \qquad (7.6)$$

The delay component T_4 is governed by elements besides the common user network and the access network parameters and does not affect the evaluation of common user networks. For the example worked out in Section 4, T_4 has been assumed to be 1 second.

The delay component T_5 can be evaluated from a knowledge of the mean of the first packet of the response and the host access line speed. Using the mean first packet length of a geometrically distributed message of mean length $1/\mu_0$ from Appendix 7B, Equation (7B4), we have

$$T_5 = \frac{1}{\mu_0 s_2} \left\{ 1 - (N+1)(1-\mu_0)^N + N(1-\mu_0)^{N+1} \right\} + \frac{N}{s_2}(1-\mu_0)^N \quad (7.7)$$

The final component of MRT, T_6, is the Mean Network Transit Delay and is the same as T_1.

7.2.3 Summary of Results

We have divided the MRT for character-at-a-time terminals communicating to a remote host over a packet switched network into six components. Two of these components (T_1 and T_6) are each the Mean Network Transit Delay, which is a typical parameter of the packet switched network. The interference delay T_2 can be evaluated using Equation (7.5). The mean host processing delay T_4 is an external parameter and is not affected by the access network configuration or the common-user-network performance.

The remaining components T_3 and T_5 are respectively governed by the mean delay of the last packet of the inquiry message and that of the first packet of the response message, and the host access line speed s_2. T_3 and T_5 are entirely governed by the user's traffic characteristics, host access line speed and the maximum packet size and can be evaluated using Equations (7.6) and (7.7) respectively. The MRT is the sum of the components T_1 through T_6.

7.3 THE BLOCK ORIENTED TERMINAL

7.3.1 Elements of End-To-End Delays

Unlike the character-at-a-time terminal, the block oriented terminal first stores the user generated information in its own buffer. After a block of information usually with a specified maximum size is ready, it is transmitted synchronously at the access line speed. Figure 7.3 depicts a block oriented terminal communicating with a remote computer or another block oriented terminal over a packet switched network.

For the inquiry-response application under consideration here, we will assume that the entire inquiry message is contained in one block. Depending upon the size of the message, however, more than one packet may be generated by the origin node for transmission to the destination node and contained in the single block.

The evaluation of MRT for block oriented terminals is carried out by subdividing it into six components T_1 through T_6.

Using the definition of MRT given in Section 7.1, it follows that in contrast to the character-at-a-time terminal, the block oriented terminal does perceive a

The Block Oriented Terminal

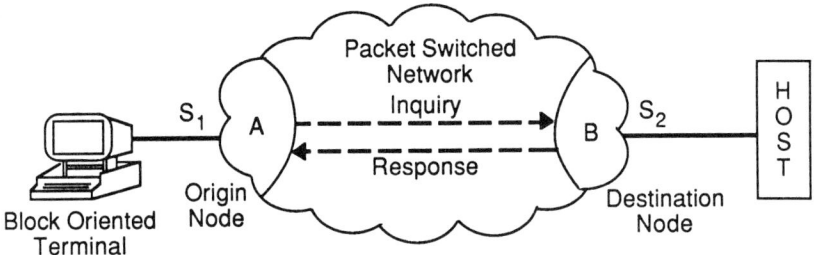

MRT Components

1. First packet-assembly delay (inquiry) at A = T_1
2. Transit delay (A to B) = T_2
3. Message transfer delay = T_3
4. Host delay = T_4
5. First packet assembly delay (response) at B = T_5
6. Cross network delay (response) B to A = T_6

Figure 7.3
Delay Components of the Block Oriented Terminal*

packetization delay at the network node interfacing the terminal. This delay is equal to the transmission delay for a number of characters that constitute the first packet of the message. Using Appendix B and assuming that the customer message parameters are the same as before, we have the packet assembly delay, Equation (7B4), given as,

$$T_1 = \frac{1}{\mu_i} s_1 \left\{ 1 - (N + 1)(1 - \mu_i)^N + N(1 - \mu_i)^{N+1} \right\} + \frac{N}{s_i}(1 - \mu_i)^N \quad (7.8)$$

The second component of MRT, T_2, will be the Mean Network Transit Delay, a performance parameter of the network.

---

* P. K. Verma, "Customer Perceived Delays in a Packet Switched Network," Proc. National Telecommunications Conf., Houston, November-December, 1980, pp. 25.1.1-25.1.5 © IEEE 1980.

The third component of MRT, T_3, will accrue at the destination node and will be the time to receive the entire message at the host access line speed by the host. Knowing the characteristics of the inquiry message, we have

$$T_3 = \frac{1}{\mu_i s_2} \tag{7.9}$$

The fourth component T_4 is the same as T_4 of the character-at-a-time terminal and is a characteristic of the host.

As discussed in Section 7.2, the response message will be blocked and packetized before being forwarded to the inquiring terminal. This packetization delay gives rise to T_5. Since the MRT involves a delay up to the receipt of the first character of the response, the statistics of the first packet of the response will determine T_5.

Using Appendix B and assuming that the response message characteristics are the same as before, we have

$$T_5 = \frac{1}{\mu_0 s_2} \left\{ 1 - (N+1)(1-\mu_0)^N + N(1-\mu_0)^{N+1} \right\}$$

$$+ \frac{n}{s_2}(1-\mu_0)^N \tag{7.10}$$

The final component of MRT, T_6, is the same as T_2.

It should be noted that the one-character delays associated with transporting the last character of the inquiry and the first character of the response have been neglected, as in the case of character-at-a-time terminals. Further, should the first response packet require a complete reassembly before being printed or displayed, a packet reassembly term similar to that for T_5 (but with s_2 replaced by s_1) will have to be used.

7.3.2 Summary of Results

The MRT for block oriented terminals has been divided into six components T_1 through T_6. Two of these components (T_3 and T_6) are each the Mean Network Transmit Delay, a characteristic performance parameter of the network. The mean host processing delay, T_4, is an external parameter reflecting the performance of the customer's host.

The remaining delay components T_1, T_3, and T_5 can be evaluated using Equations (7.8), (7.9), and (7.10) respectively. The MRT is the sum of the components T_1 through T_6.

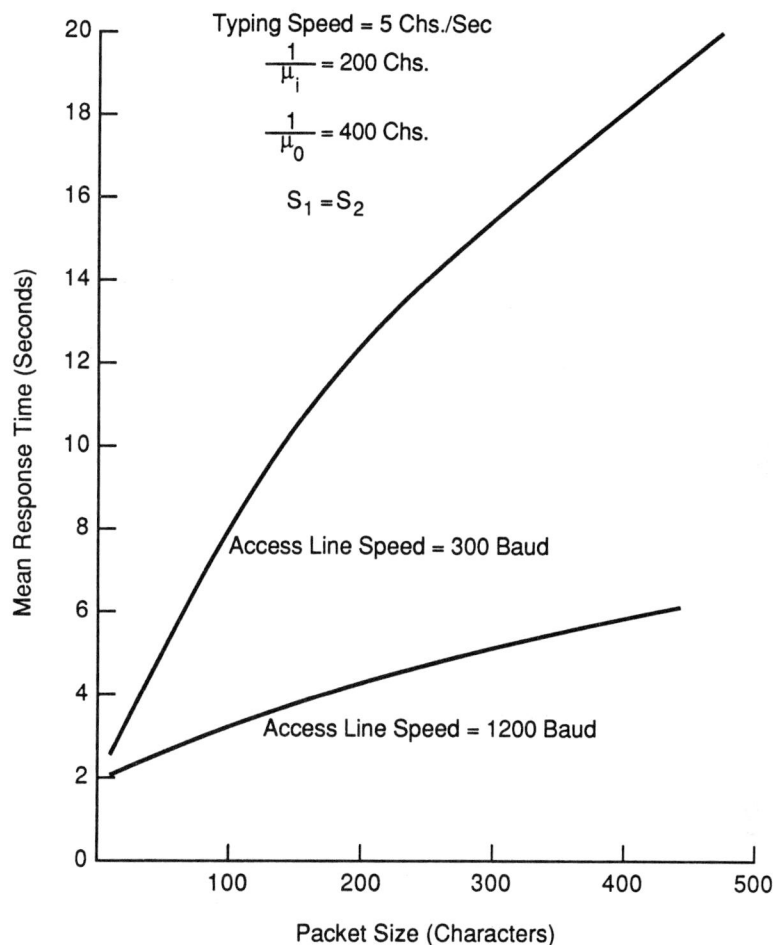

Figure 7.4
Packet Size vs Mean Response Time
Character-at-a-Time Terminal*

---

* P. K. Verma, "Customer Perceived Delays in a Packet Switched Network," Proc. National Telecommunications Conf., Houston, November-December, 1980, pp. 25.1.1-25.1.5 © IEEE 1980.

7.4 NUMERICAL RESULTS

Figures 7.4 and 7.5 illustrate the dependence of the Mean Response Time on the packet size. In each case the inquiry and the response messages are

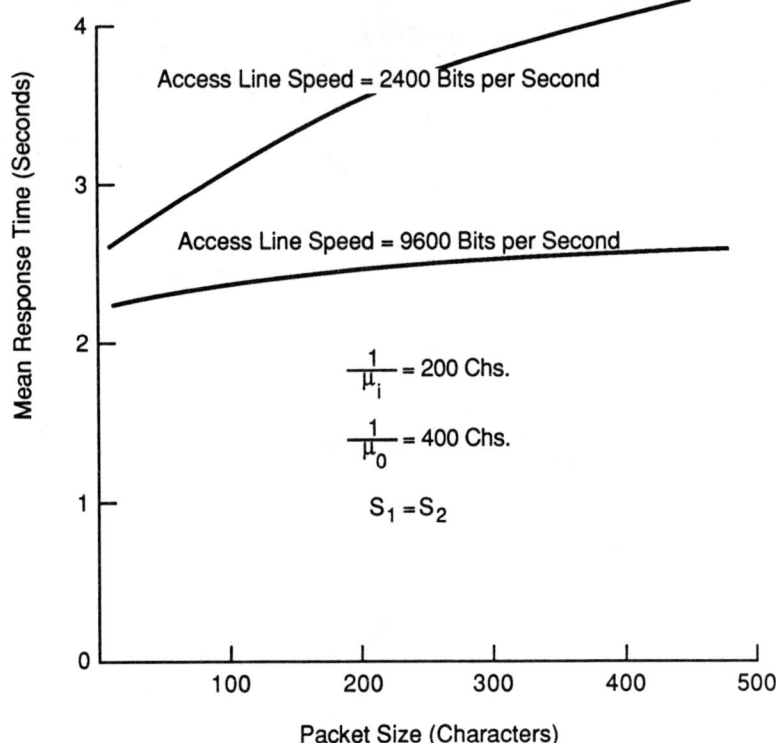

Figure 7.5
Packet Size vs Mean Response Time
Block Oriented Terminal*

geometrically distributed with means of 200 and 400 characters respectively. For the character-at-a-time terminal, the typing speed (which affects the delay component T_2) has been assumed to be 5 characters per second.

---

* P. K. Verma, "Customer Perceived Delays in a Packet Switched Network," Proc. National Telecommunications Conf., Houston, November-December, 1980, pp. 25.1.1-25.1.5 © IEEE 1980.

The heavy dependence of MRT on the maximum packet size can be noted from Figure 7.4. For block oriented terminals at high speed, this effect is minimal.

7.5 MESSAGE ASSEMBLY PROTOCOLS AND END-TO-END DELAYS

7.5.1 The Influence of Message Assembly Protocols on End-to-End Delays

In the two situations that we studied for determining the MRT for the character-at-a-time terminal and the block oriented terminal, we did not require that the message in its entirety be received by the network either at the entry or the exit node before being forwarded to the next node or to the user's equipment. Recall that it is the message that has significance at the user level. The packetizing of messages must be viewed as a process which permits an efficient usage of the network by users with a variety of applications and traffic characteristics.

It is thus entirely possible that a packet switched network may adopt a protocol that requires the nodes of entry and exit to operate on the message as a whole. In other words, the node of entry will receive the entire message, consisting of several packets, before forwarding it to the next network node. Similarly, the exit node may reassemble the entire message (again, consisting potentially of several packets) before forwarding it to the user's terminal or host. In order to illustrate the effect of the various combinations of the message assembly protocols on the user perceived delay, consider the model and the analysis in the following sections.

7.5.2 The Model

Consider a block oriented terminal communicating to a remote host across a packet switched network as shown, for example, in Figure 7.3. After a block of information with usually a specified maximum size is ready, it is transmitted at the access line speed s_1. Assume again that the entire message is contained in one block. Depending upon its size, however, the message may result in more than one packet being transmitted. Consider two possible variances of protocol at the node of entry: If protocol P_1 is adopted, the entire message will be received by the network before the first packet is transmitted toward the destination. With the use of protocol P_2, the node will dispatch a packet as soon as it is received in its entirety at the node of entry. (Note that in the case of single-packet messages, the receipt of the first packet at the node of entry also results in the entire message being received.)

Protocols P_3 and P_4 used at the exit node are analogous to the protocols P_1 and P_2 at the entry node, respectively. Use of protocol P_3 will thus require the message being reconstituted in its entirety within the network before the first packet exits toward the destination terminal. On the other hand, use of protocol P_4 will permit the first packet to exit as soon as it has been received in its entirety, rather than requiring it to wait for the subsequent packets of this same message, if any. For each message traversing the network, a choice between two protocols, P_1 and P_2, at the node of entry and between two protocols, P_3 and P_4, at the node of exit, are possible. I now assess the delay inside the packet switched network induced on account of each of the four possible combinations of protocols at the entry and exit nodes, namely, P_1P_3, P_1P_4, P_2P_3, and P_2P_4.

7.5.3 Analysis

We are interested in evaluating the network delay induced by adopting each of the four protocol combinations mentioned above. Specifically, the delay components addressed here are: (i) delay suffered at the node of entry by requiring that either the first packet or the entire message be blocked before it is allowed to proceed toward the exit node, and (ii) delay suffered at the exit node by requiring that either the first packet or the entire message be blocked before it exits the network toward the destination terminal. The end-to-end delay perceived by the user on account of message assembly at either the entry or the exit node will be equal to the delay experienced by the entire message or the first packet (at the applicable line speed), depending upon whether message assembly protocol (P_1 or P_2) and (P_3 or P_4) was adopted.

We assume that the user message with a mean length of $1/\mu_1$ is geometrically distributed, that is, the probability function $P_1(m)$ of the message can be expressed as:

$$P_1(m) = \mu_1(1 - \mu_1)^{m-1} \quad m=1, 2, 3, \ldots \tag{7.11}$$

Case 1: Use of Protocol Pair P_1P_3

As noted previously, use of protocol pair P_1P_3 will require the entire message to be fully assembled at both the entry and the destination nodes. Accordingly, the probability function for delay equal to $(m/s_1 + m/s_2)$ will be given by:

$$P_2(m/s_1 + m/s_2) = \mu_1(1 - \mu_1)^{m-1} \quad m = 1, 2, 3, \ldots \tag{7.12}$$

The mean delay D_1 can be evaluated as:

$$D_1 = \sum_{m=1}^{\infty} \left[\frac{m}{s_1} + \frac{m}{s_2}\right]\mu_1\left(1-\mu_1\right)^{m-1}$$

$$= \mu_1\left[\frac{1}{s_1} + \frac{1}{s_2}\right]\sum_{m=1}^{\infty} m\left(1-\mu_1\right)^{m-1}$$

$$= \mu_1\left[\frac{1}{s_1} + \frac{1}{s_2}\right]\frac{d}{d\left(1-\mu_1\right)}\sum_{m=1}^{\infty}\left(1-\mu_1\right)^m$$

$$= \mu_1\left[\frac{1}{s_1} + \frac{1}{s_2}\right]\frac{1}{\mu_1^2}$$

$$= \frac{1}{\mu_1 s_1} + \frac{1}{\mu_1 s_2} \tag{7.13}$$

after some algebraic simplifications.

Case 2: Use of Protocol Pair $P_1 P_4$

In this case, the entire message will be assembled at the entry node. However, at the exit node, the message will start exiting as soon as the first packet has been received in full.

Given the statistics of the message in Equation (7.11), the statistics of the first packet can be given from (7B3) as:

$$P_3(k) = \mu_1\left(1-\mu_1\right)^{k-1} \quad k < N \tag{7.14}$$

$$= \left(1-\mu_1\right)^{N-1} \quad k = N$$

The probability of delay being equal to $\left[\dfrac{m}{s_1} + \dfrac{k}{s_2}\right]$ can be given as:

$$P_4\left[\frac{m}{s_1}+\frac{m}{s_2}\right]=\mu_1\left[1-\mu_1\right]^{m-1} \quad m=1,2,3,\ldots N-1$$

$$P_4'\left[\frac{m}{s_1}+\frac{N}{s_2}\right]=\mu_1\left[1-\mu_1\right]^{m-1} \quad m\geq N \qquad (7.15)$$

The mean delay D_2 can now be evaluated as:

$$D_2=\sum_{m=1}^{N-1}\left[\frac{m}{s_1}+\frac{m}{s_2}\right]\mu_1\left[1-\mu_1\right]^{m-1}$$

$$+\sum_{m=N}^{\infty}\left[\frac{m}{s_1}+\frac{N}{s_2}\right]\mu_1\left[1-\mu_1\right]^{m-1} \qquad (7.16)$$

(7.16) can be simplified as:

$$D_2=\sum_{m=1}^{\infty}\frac{m}{s_1}\mu_1\left[1-\mu_1\right]^{m-1}+\sum_{m=1}^{N-1}\frac{m}{s_2}\mu_1\left[1-\mu_1\right]^{m-1}$$

$$+\sum_{m=N}^{\infty}\frac{N}{s_2}\mu_1\left[1-\mu_1\right]^{m-1}$$

$$=\frac{1}{\mu_1 s_1}+\frac{1-\left[N+1\right]\left[1-\mu_1\right]^N+N\left[1-\mu_1\right]^{N+1}}{\mu_1 s_2}$$

$$+\frac{N\left[1-\mu_1\right]^N}{s_2} \qquad (7.17)$$

after some algebraic simplifications.

Case 3: Use of Protocol Pair P_2P_3

In this case, only the first packet will be blocked at the node of entry, but the entire message will have to be assembled at the exit node.

From a study of Case 2, the probability of delay being equal to $\left(\dfrac{k}{s_1} + \dfrac{m}{s_2}\right)$ can be given as:

$$P_5\left(\dfrac{m}{s_1} + \dfrac{m}{s_2}\right) = \mu_1\left(1 - \mu_1\right)^{m-1} \quad m = 1, 2, 3, \ldots, N-1$$

$$P'_5\left(\dfrac{N}{s_1} + \dfrac{m}{s_2}\right) = \mu_1\left(1 - \mu_1\right)^{m-1} \quad m \geq N \tag{7.18}$$

Following the same procedure as in Case 2, the mean delay D_3 can be evaluated as:

$$D_3 = \dfrac{1}{\mu_1 s_2} + \dfrac{1 - [N+1]\left(1 - \mu_1\right)^N + N\left(1 - \mu_1\right)^{N+1}}{\mu_1 s_1}$$

$$+ \dfrac{N\left(1 - \mu_1\right)^N}{s_2} \tag{7.19}$$

Case 4: Use of Protocol Pair $P_2 P_4$

In this case, only the first packet will be blocked at both the entry and the exit nodes. Using the same approach as before, the probability that delay will be being equal to $\left[\dfrac{m}{s_1} + \dfrac{m}{s_2}\right]$ can be given as:

$$P_6\left(\dfrac{m}{s_1} + \dfrac{m}{s_2}\right) = \mu_1\left(1 - \mu_1\right)^{m-1} \quad m = 1, 2, 3, \ldots, N-1$$

$$P'_6\left(\dfrac{N}{s_1} + \dfrac{N}{s_2}\right) = \mu_1\left(1 - \mu_1\right)^{m-1} \quad m \geq N \tag{7.20}$$

The mean delay D_4 can be evaluated as:

$$D_4 = \sum_{m=1}^{n-1} \left[\frac{m}{s_1} + \frac{m}{s_2} \right] \mu_1 \left(1 - \mu_1\right)^{m-1} + \left[\frac{N}{s_1} + \frac{N}{s_2} \right] \sum_{m=N}^{\infty} \mu_1 \left(1 - \mu_1\right)^{m-1}$$

$$= \mu_1 \left[\frac{1}{s_1} + \frac{1}{s_2} \right] \sum_{m=1}^{N-1} m \left(1 - \mu_1\right)^{m-1} + N \left[\frac{1}{s_1} + \frac{1}{s_2} \right] \sum_{m=N}^{\infty} \mu_1 \left(1 - \mu_1\right)^{m-1}$$

$$= \frac{1}{\mu_1} \left[\frac{1}{s_1} + \frac{1}{s_2} \right] \left\{ 1 - (N+1)\left(1 - \mu_1\right)^N + N\left(1 - \mu_1\right)^{N+1} \right\}$$

$$+ \left[\frac{1}{s_1} + \frac{1}{s_2} \right] N \left(1 - \mu_1\right)^N \qquad (7.21)$$

7.5.4 Numerical Results

A comparison of the four assembly protocols can now be effected. We examine the following cases:

Case I:

  $s_1 = s_2 = 300$ bits per second

  $N = 128$ and 256 characters

Case II:

  $s_1 = 300$ bits per second

  $s_2 = 1200$ bits per second

  $N = 128$ and 256 characters

Figures 7.6 and 7.7 illustrate Case I for maximum packet sizes of 128 and 256 characters, respectively. Similarly, Figures 7.8 and 7.9 illustrate Case II for maximum packet sizes of 128 and 256 characters, respectively. (A character is assumed to consist of 8 bits).

In Case I, where the line speeds s_1 and s_2 are equal, it can be readily observed that protocol options P_1P_4 and P_2P_3 (Figures 7.6 and 7.7) present identical average delays for each parameter set (s_1, s_2, N). This can be readily shown to be true from Equations (7.17) and (7.19) which will yield the same value whenever $s_1 = s_2$. Under protocol option P_1P_3, where the entire

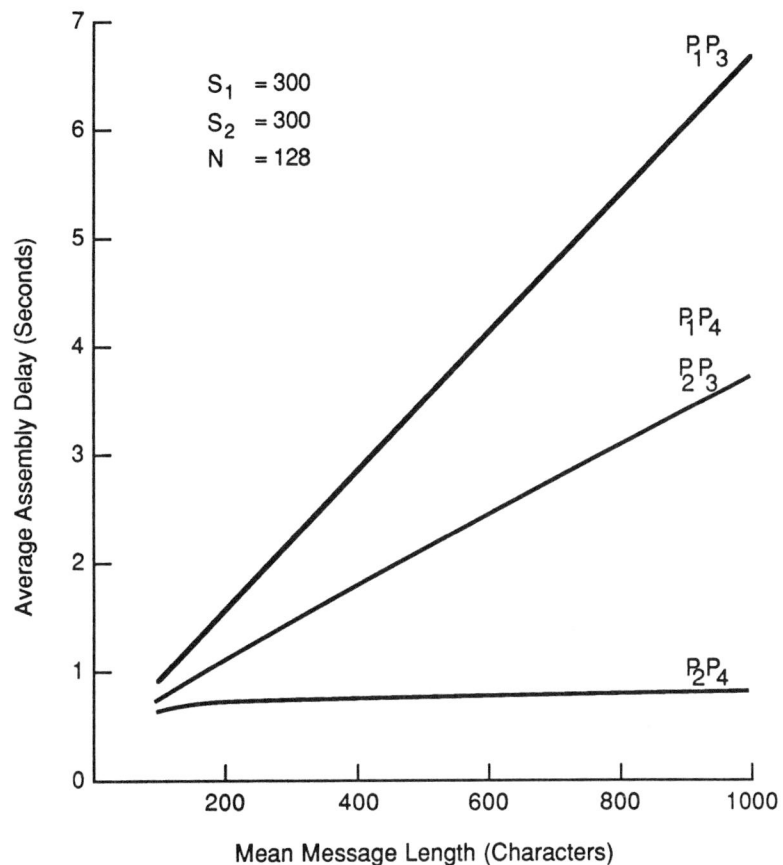

Figure 7.6
Average Assembly Delay vs Mean Message Length
Case I, N = 128

message is fully assembled at both the entry and exit nodes, the average protocol delay is independent of the maximum packet size permitted in the network. The protocol option P_2P_4 presents the least delay alternative in both Figures 7.6 and 7.7; however, this option is also the one most sensitive to the maximum packet size chosen. As $1/\mu_1$ is increased indefinitely, it can be readily shown from Equation (7.3) that D_4 asymptotically reaches the value $N(1/s_1 + 1/s_2)$. This also follows from physical considerations since the maximum delay suffered at either the entry or the exit node, under this option, is limited to that experienced by a single packet at the applicable line speed. The average delays associated with protocol options P_1P_4 and P_2P_3 lie between the options P_1P_3 and P_2P_4. It can be observed that, unlike the P_2P_4 case, average delays in the P_1P_3 and P_1P_4 or P_2P_3 cases are not bounded as the mean message length is increased.

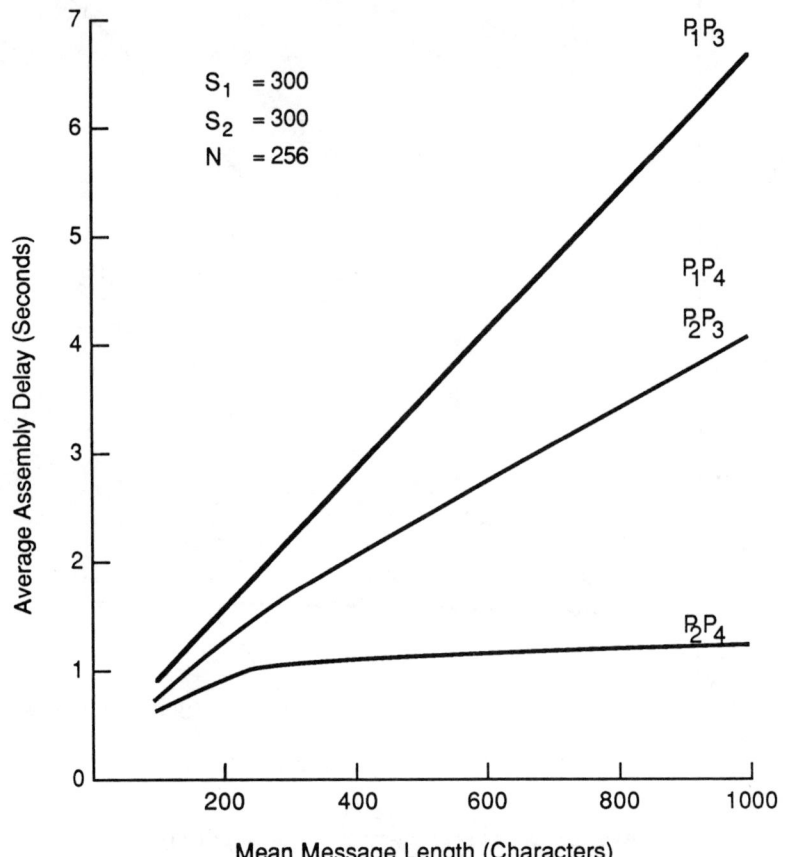

Figure 7.7
Average Assembly Delay vs Mean Message Length
Case I, N = 256

Figures 7.8 and 7.9 represent Case II for $N = 128$ and $N = 256$ respectively. Here, the same observations as in the previous case can be made. However, since $s_1 \neq s_2$ here, protocol options P_1P_4 and P_2P_3 do not present identical delays for any given parameter set (s_1, s_2, N). Since $s_2 > s_1$, a full message assembly at node A, instead of at node B, will be always more penalizing in terms of protocol delays. This is shown by the P_1P_4 curve being consistently higher than the P_2P_3 curve. The delay represented by the P_2P_4 curve is bounded, as in Case I, to the same limit $N\left[1/s_1 + 1/s_2\right]$.

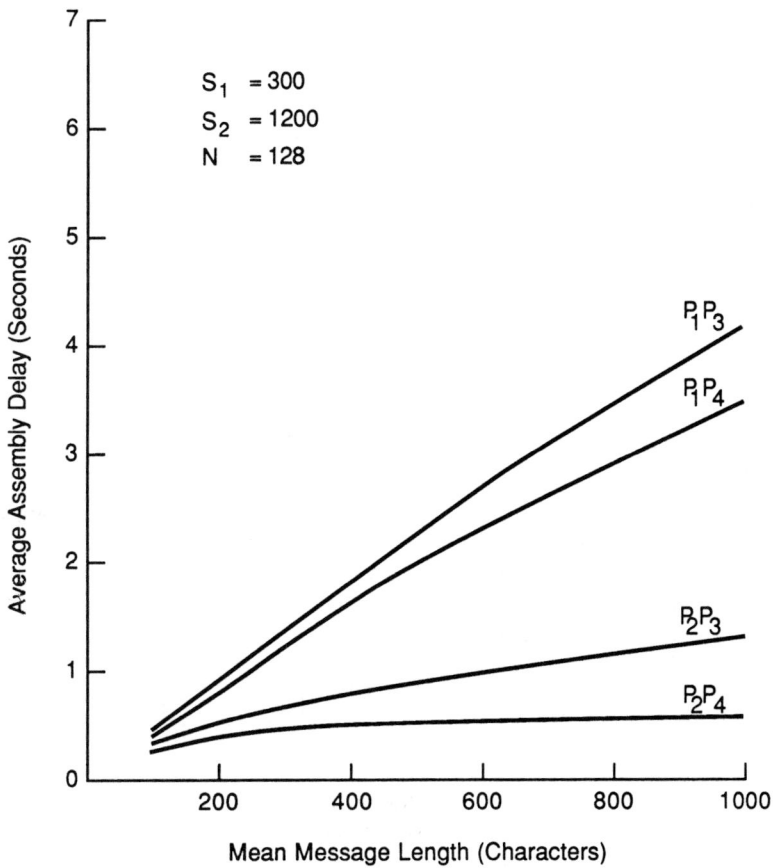

Figure 7.8
Average Assembly Delay vs Mean Message Length
Case II, N = 128

7.6 PERCENTILE RESPONSE TIMES [8]

So far, we have derived expressions for the Mean Response Time perceived by a packet switched network customer with an inquiry-response application. Both character-at-a-time and block oriented terminals have been considered.

It has been shown that for most cases of practical interest, the access line speed wields considerable influence in determining customer perceived delays.

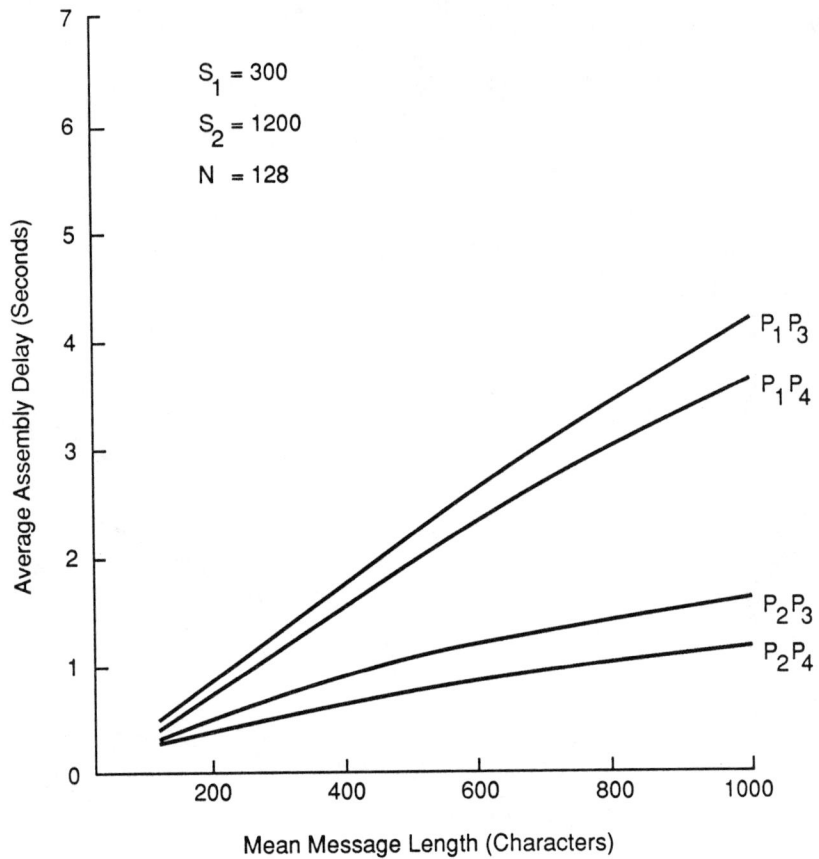

Figure 7.9
Average Assembly Delay vs Mean Message Length
Case II, N = 256

As stated earlier, the estimation of percentile response times is of crucial importance in a number of interactive applications. Unfortunately, the response time is usually composed of a number of components each with a distribution of its own, making the computation of any parameter other than the mean somewhat difficult. In the most general case, some of these components may be continuous variables and the others discrete variables. The situation defies the use of conventional Laplace transform techniques. A typical example of the situation discussed here arises in the end-to-end delay analysis of a packet switched network, where some of the components can be modeled as continuous variables and the others as discrete variables.

I propose here a methodology to derive the tail-end distribution of the composite response time using a combination of the Laplace transform inversion techniques and convolution techniques. The proposed method is direct and no assumptions (other than the mutual independence of each of the component variables) or approximations are involved. The mutual independence assumption appears better justified here than in the conventional analysis of internodal delays. The reasons are attributable to the modeling approach we have adopted here by coalescing all intranetwork delays into one delay component and having the network independent-access delays and customer equipment delays as other components.

The mathematical foundation of the method is described in Section 7.7. Section 7.8 presents an example of application of the method.

7.7 THE PROPOSED METHOD

Let $f_1(t), f_2(t), \ldots, f_n(t)$ be the probability density functions of those components of the response time that are continuous variables. A typical example of such a density function is the exponential probability density function:

$$\left. \begin{array}{ll} f_i(t) = ae^{-at} & t > 0 \\ = 0 & t \leq 0 \end{array} \right\} \qquad (7.22)$$

Let $P_1(k), P_2(k), \ldots, P_m(k) \ldots$ be the probability distribution functions of the discrete components of the response time, that is, let

$$P_i(k) = \text{Prob}\left[\text{Delay} = \frac{k}{Q}\right] \qquad (7.23)$$

where, $k = 1, 2, 3, \ldots$ and Q is a scaling factor.

The suggested procedure consists in first obtaining one composite distribution for the continuous functions and another for the discrete functions.

Let $F_i(s)$ be the Laplace transform of the ith continuous function;

$$F_i(s) = \int_0^\infty f_i(t)e^{-st}dt \qquad (7.24)$$

Then, we have the Laplace transform of the composite continuous distribution functions given as [9]:

$$F_c(s) = \prod_{i=1}^{n} F_i(s) \qquad (7.25)$$

Usually, it will be possible to invert $F_c(s)$ so as to obtain the corresponding time domain probability density function $f_c(t)$, that is,

$$f_c(t) = \frac{1}{2\Pi i} \int_{a-i\infty}^{a+i\infty} F_c(s)e^{st} ds \qquad (7.26)$$

where $s = a + iw$ is the complex variable. If $F_c(s)$ cannot be inverted by using one of the standard inversion techniques (such as partial fraction expansion), a numerical inversion procedure is suggested [10].

From Equation (7.26), the probability distribution function of the composite continuous functions can be obtained as

$$F_c(t) = \int_0^t f_c(t) dt \cdots \qquad (7.27)$$

The tail-end distribution (i.e., the probability that the delay is greater than or equal to t) is given by:

$$F_c^1(t) = 1 - \int_0^t f_c(t) dt \cdots \qquad (7.28)$$

Now consider the discrete variables with distributions given by $P_1(k), P_2(k), \ldots, P_m(k)$. A convolution [9] of all the discrete distribution functions represented as:

$$H(k) = P_1(k) * P_2(k) * P_3(k) \ldots P_m(k) \qquad (7.29)$$

furnishes the distribution function of the arithmetic sum of the component variables. If P_i is defined for N_i discrete values of k, then H_k will be defined for $\sum_{i=1}^{m} N_i - (m-1)$ values of k. Assume further that a value k of the composite discrete variable occurring with the probability $H(k)$ results in a delay of K/Q, where Q is a scaling factor.

From equations (7.28) and (7.29) one can now write the probability of the overall delay being equal to or greater than τ or $P_0(D \geq \tau)$ as:

$$P_0(D \geq \tau) = \sum_{k=m}^{\sum_{i=1}^{n} Ni} F_c^1\left\{\tau - \frac{k}{Q}\right\} H(k) \qquad (7.30)$$

with the stipulation that

$$F_c^1(i) = 1 \quad \text{for } i \leq 0$$

(7.30) gives the required distribution function.

7.8 A CASE STUDY

As an example of the procedure suggested above, consider a situation where the response time has five components, three of which are continuous variables and the remaining two discrete. The probability functions of the components are defined below. Note that the first two continuous variables are identically distributed. We have

$$f_1(\tau) = \alpha e^{-\alpha \tau}$$

$$f_2(\tau) = \alpha e^{-\alpha \tau}$$

$$f_3(\tau) = \beta e^{-\beta \tau}$$

$$P_1(k) = \frac{\mu_1(1-\mu_1)^{k-1}}{1-(1-\mu_1)^N} \quad k = 1, 2, \ldots, N$$

$$P_2(k) = \mu(1-\mu_1)^{k-1} \quad k = 1, 2, \ldots, N-1$$

$$= N(1-\mu_1)^{N-1} \quad k = N$$

The numerical parameters are defined as follows:

$$\alpha = 3.3333333 \text{ sec}^{-1}$$
$$\beta = 1 \text{ sec}^{-1}$$
$$N = 100$$
$$\frac{1}{\mu_1} = 200 \quad \text{characters}$$

Assume further that a value k of the discrete variable results in a delay $k/30$ seconds (i.e., $Q = 30$).

Using Equation (7.24), we have

$$\left. \begin{aligned} F_1(s) &= \frac{\alpha}{s + \alpha} \\ F_2(s) &= \frac{\alpha}{s + \alpha} \\ F_3(s) &= \frac{\beta}{s + \beta} \end{aligned} \right\} \quad (7.31)$$

and from Equation (7.25), we obtain

$$F_c(s) = \left[\frac{\alpha}{s + \alpha} \right]^2 \frac{\beta}{s + \beta} \quad (7.32)$$

Using expansion by partial fractions, we obtain from Equation (7.32)

$$F_c(s) = \left[\frac{\alpha}{\alpha - \beta} \right]^2 \frac{\beta}{s + \beta} - \alpha \frac{\beta}{(\alpha - \beta)^2} \frac{\alpha}{s + \alpha} + \frac{\beta}{\beta - \alpha} \left[\frac{\alpha}{s + \alpha} \right]^2 \quad (7.33)$$

Using standard Laplace inversion techniques [9], we now obtain

$$f_c(\tau) = \left[\frac{\alpha}{\alpha - \beta} \right]^2 \beta e^{-\beta \tau} - \alpha \frac{\beta}{(\alpha - \beta)^2} \alpha e^{-\alpha \tau} + \frac{\beta}{\beta - \alpha} \alpha^2 \tau e^{-\alpha \tau} \quad (7.34)$$

A Case Study

The distribution function $F_c(\tau)$ can be obtained from Equation (7.34) as follows:

$$F_c(\tau) = \left[\frac{\alpha}{\alpha - \beta}\right]^2 \left[1 - e^{-\beta\tau}\right] - \alpha \frac{\beta}{(\alpha - \beta)^2} \left[1 - e^{-\alpha\tau}\right]$$

$$+ \frac{\beta}{\beta - \alpha}\left[1 - e^{-\alpha\tau}(1 + \alpha\tau)\right]$$

$$= 1 - \left[\frac{\alpha}{\alpha - \beta}\right]^2 e^{-\beta\tau} + \alpha \frac{\beta}{(\alpha - \beta)^2} e^{-\alpha\tau}$$

$$+ \frac{\beta}{\alpha - \beta} e^{-\alpha\tau}(1 + \alpha\tau)$$

$$= 1 - \frac{\alpha^2}{(\alpha - \beta)^2} e^{-\beta\tau} + \left[\frac{2\alpha\beta - \beta^2}{(\alpha - \beta)^2} + \frac{\alpha}{\alpha - \beta}\tau\right] e^{-\alpha\tau} \quad (7.35)$$

From Equation (7.24), the tail-end distribution can be written as:

$$\text{Prob(Delay} \geq \tau) = F_1^c(\tau) = 1 - F_c(\tau)$$

$$= \frac{\alpha^2}{(\alpha - \beta)^2} e^{-\beta\tau} - \left[\frac{2\alpha\beta - \beta^2}{(\alpha - \beta)^2} + \alpha\frac{\beta}{\alpha - \beta}\tau\right] e^{-\alpha\tau} \quad (7.36)$$

Now consider the discrete functions $P_1(k)$ and $P_2(k)$. If we convolve these two sequences (each with N values) then we shall obtain a new sequence $H(k)$ with $(2N - 1)$ values. The sequence $H(k)$ shall give the probability that the sum of two discrete delay components will have the value k. Mathematically,

$$H(k) = P(k)*Q(k)$$

or

$$H(k) = \sum_{j=0}^{k} P(k - j)Q(j) \quad k = 2, 3, \ldots, 2N \quad (7.37)$$

with the stipulation that

$$H(i), P(i), Q(i) = 0 \quad i \leq 0$$

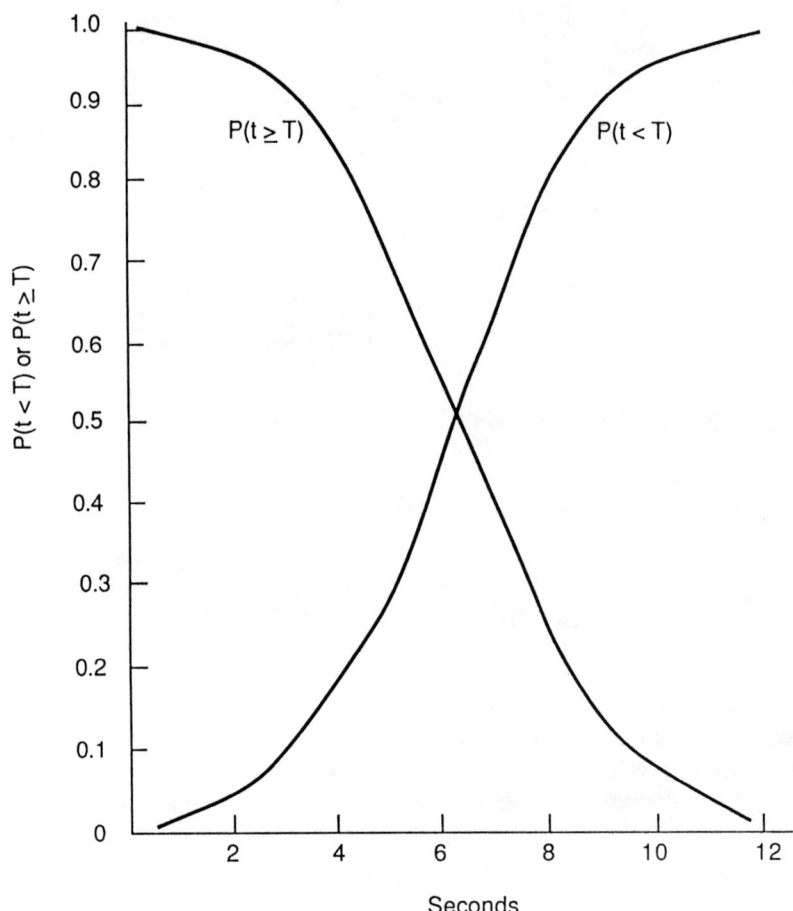

Figure 7.10
Response Time T^*

---

* P. K. Verma, "A Procedure for Estimating Percentile Response Time in a Packet Switched Network," Proc. Int. Conf. on Comm., Seattle, June 1980, pp. 61.5.1-61.5.4 © IEEE 1980.

Appendix 7A

If a value k of the resultant discrete variable results in a delay of k/Q seconds, (where Q is the scaling factor), then the probability $P_0(D \geq \tau)$ that the overall delay is equal to or greater than τ is given by

$$P_0(D \geq \tau) = \sum_{k=2}^{2N} F_c^1\left[\tau - \frac{k}{Q}\right] H(k) \qquad (7.38)$$

with the stipulation that

$$F_c^1(i) = 1 \quad i = 0$$

Using the values of parameters α, β, N and $1/\mu_1$ defined earlier and using the scaling factor $Q = 30$, $P_0(D \geq \tau)$ can be readily computed. The same is illustrated in Figure 7.10.

In summary, Sections 7.7 and 7.8 have presented an application of the existing mathematical tools for evaluating the distribution of the response time in a packet switched network. The occurrence of both continuous and discrete components in the response time is permissible. The proposed method is simple and direct and no assumption other than the mutual independence of the component variables is essential.

7.9 APPENDIX 7A

7.9.1 Statistics of the Last Packet of a Geometrically Distributed Message

The probability function $P_1(m)$ of the message can be expressed as:

$$P_1(m) = \mu_1(1-\mu_1)^{m-1} \quad m = 1, 2, 3\ldots \qquad (7A1)$$

Let the maximum packet size be N and let the length of the last packet be k, $(k \leq m, N)$, then we have $P_2(k)$, the probability function of the last packet, given as,

$$P_2(k) = \sum_{j=0}^{\infty} P_1(k + jN) \quad 1 \leq k \leq N$$

$$= \frac{\mu_1(1-\mu_1)^{k-1}}{1-(1-\mu_1)^N} \quad 1 \leq k \leq N \qquad (7A2)$$

Let $\frac{1}{\mu_2}$ be the mean of the last packet. Then,

$$\frac{1}{\mu_2} = \sum_{k=1}^{N} k P_2(k)$$

$$= \frac{\mu_1}{1-(1-\mu_1)^N} \sum_{k=1}^{N} k(1-\mu_1)^{k-1} \qquad (7A3)$$

Using some algebraic simplifications, (7A3) can be simplified to yield

$$\frac{1}{\mu_2} = \frac{1-(N+1)(1-\mu_1)^N + N(1-\mu_1)^{N+1}}{\mu_1\{1-(1-\mu_1)^N\}} \qquad (7A4)$$

7.10 APPENDIX 7B

7.10.1 Statistics of the First Packet of a Geometrically Distributed Message

As in Appendix 7A, we have

$$P_1(m) = \mu_1(1-\mu_1)^{m-1} \quad m = 1, 2, 3, \ldots \qquad (7B1)$$

Assuming k to be the variable representing the length of the first packet, we have the probability function of the first packet given as;

$$P_2(k) = \mu_1(1-\mu_1)^{k-1} \quad k < N$$

$$= \sum_{N}^{\infty} \mu_1(1-\mu_1)^{k-1} \quad k = N \qquad (7B2)$$

(7B2) can be simplified as:

$$P_2(k) = \mu_1(1-\mu_1)^{k-1} \quad k < N$$

$$= (1-\mu_1)^{N-1} \quad k = N \qquad (7B3)$$

The mean of the first packet can now be written as:

$$\frac{1}{\mu_2} = \sum_{k=1}^{N-1} k\mu_1(1-\mu_1)^{k-1} + N(1-\mu_1)^{N-1}$$

$$= \frac{1}{\mu_1}\left\{1 - (N+1)(1-\mu_1)^N + N(1-\mu_1)^{N+1}\right\} + N(1-\mu_1)^N \quad (7B4)$$

after some algebraic simplifications.

7.11 REFERENCES

[1] I. Rubin, "Message Path Delays in Packet-Switching Communication Networks," IEEE Trans. on Comm., Vol. Com-23, No. 2, February 1975, pp. 186-192.

[2] R. N. Pandya, "Delay Analysis for Datapack — A Packet Switched Network with two Priority Classes," Proc. of the Fifth Data Comm. Symposium, September 1977, pp. 3-14 through 3-21.

[3] H. Miyahara, Y. Texhigawara, and T. Rasegawa, Delay and Throughput Evaluation of Switching Methods in Computer Communications Networks," IEEE Trans. on Comm., Vol. Com-26, No. 3, March 1978, pp. 337-344.

[4] J. Chammas, "Response Times Over Packet Switched Networks — Some Performance Issues," Proc. Sixth Int. Conf. on Computer Comm., London, September 1982, pp. 993-998.

[5] D. Sproule and M. Unsoy, "Transit Delay Objectives for the Datapac Network," Proc. Fifth Int. Conf. on Computer Comm., Atlanta, Oct 1980, pp. 685-692.

[6] P. K. Verma, "Customer Perceived Delays in a Packet Switched Network," Proc. National Telecommunications Conf., Houston, November - December 1980, pp. 25.1.1-25.1.5.

[7] S. M. Lauretti, "Users: See For Yourselves How Public Data Nets Perform," Data Communications, January 1987, pp. 104-117.

[8] P. K. Verma, "A Procedure for Estimating Percentile Response Time in a Packet Switched Network," Proc. Int. Conf. on Comm., Seattle, June 1980, pp. 61.5.1-61.5.4.

[9] C. R. Wylie, *Advanced Engineering Mathematics*, McGraw-Hill, New York, 1975, Chapter 7.

[10] D. L. Jagerman, "An Inversion Technique for the Laplace Transform with Application to Approximation," Bell System Technical Journal, Vol. 57, No. 3., March 1978, pp 669-710.

Chapter 8

PERFORMANCE OBJECTIVES

Performance objectives are goals that have been identified using some criteria of optimality. This chapter considers the basis for deriving performance objectives from an engineering standpoint. An example is furnished to illustrate this point.

8.1 NEED FOR PERFORMANCE OBJECTIVES

We have seen in Chapter 2 that two or more systems performing identical functions are differentiated in terms of their performance. The performance of a system is described using an applicable set of performance parameters. The numerical values of the parameters are also referred to as performance levels. Performance objectives are target values of the performance parameters under specified operational conditions.

The design and development phase of a computer communication network or system is often preceded by a set of performance specifications. Specifications are the minimum acceptable levels of performance from the end user's perspective. For example, a computer communication network used for on-line credit checking may be specified in terms of the average cross-network delay being, say, no more than 300 milliseconds. Additionally, a percentile statistics may be given, or confidence levels in the statistics may be furnished. User-level specifications are written based on considerations of the particular application, which in turn originates from tolerance levels of the individuals using the system.

As discussed in Chapter 5, performance can usually be enhanced by incurring additional costs. From an engineering perspective, the optimum value of the performance objective is based on the trade-off between the rate at which performance improves and cost. Of course, this trade-off is applied only after the minimum performance requirements of the application under consideration have been met.

8.2 MAJOR DETERMINANTS OF PERFORMANCE OBJECTIVES

The trade-off the system designer has to consider in specifying a certain level of performance as the goal (i.e., the performance objective) is often complex and judgmental. Whenever, and to whatever extent, a given user specification could be exceeded without incurring additional cost, it obviously makes sense to do so. Beyond this, the system designer must evaluate whether the additional cost associated with exceeding specifications will be worth it from the end user's perspective. A point should be made that the initial goals of performance furnished by the user can usually be changed by the system designer based on the performance-cost trade-off. In other words, customers' desires for user perceived parameters must be tempered by the performance-cost characteristics of the system as a whole.

The field of computer communication networks, and indeed the entire field of information technology, exists in a highly competitive and dynamic environment. What may seem to be an adequate performance level today may become so poor — relatively speaking — in a short span of time, as to render the system useless before its design life is over. This calls for informed judgements on the part of system designers in choosing performance objectives from a given set of performance specifications. The system designer is guided by two factors in the process of making his or her choice. He or she must understand customers' expectations and the extent of their ability to pay a higher price for higher levels of performance. Further, the system designer must also understand the relationship between the cost of incorporating additional technology to enhance performance and the extent of improvement in the performance level thus made possible.

Under certain idealized conditions, it may be possible to compute optimum levels of performance objectives. I illustrate such a procedure in the following section.

8.3 RELATIONSHIP BETWEEN PERFORMANCE PARAMETERS

As discussed before, a system is usually described from a performance perspective in terms of a number of parameters, rather than a single parameter. We assume for purposes of the following analysis that these parameters are independent; in other words, enhancement of one parameter value does not affect performance levels as described in terms of the remaining parameters.* Under the above conditions, we intend to answer the following question: Is there any way to derive an optimum value of the performance parameter or values of the set of parameters that together constitute the performance objective. In other words, how should the system designer allocate his or her total "performance dollars" into setting the optimum values of the objectives for each of the performance parameters?

Let us define a parameter U reflecting the utility or value of the system. For example, if the system being considered is a transmission medium, its utility may simply be the residual throughput for a certain class of application. If the system functionality is pre-specified and fixed, utility is simply a function of the system performance parameters, $p_1, p_2, \ldots, p_n$. In other words,

$$U = f(p_1, p_2, \ldots, p_n) \tag{8.1}$$

Assume further, without loss of generality, that increases in the p_i's correspond to higher or more desirable levels of performance. Mathematically, this implies

$$\frac{\delta U}{\delta p_i} > 0 \tag{8.2}$$

Enhancements in the system utility can thus be accomplished by enhancing any of the p_i's.

Let C_i be the cost associated with the performance level p_i. An incremental enhancement δp_i would necessitate an additional expenditure δC_i.

Naturally,

$$\frac{\delta p_i}{\delta C_i} > 0 \tag{8.3}$$

Notice that the quantity $\delta U/\delta p_i$ is the marginal utility of the parameter p_i. Similarly, $\delta C_i/\delta p_i$ is the marginal price of the parameter p_i. The ratio of the marginal utility of parameter p_i to its (i.e., p_i's) marginal price is thus given by

---

* We must point out that in reality this is seldom the case. The procedure discussed here can nevertheless be successfully applied in several situations.

$$\frac{\delta U / \delta p_i}{\delta C_i / \delta p_i} \qquad (8.4)$$

When the relationship between the different parameters is optimum, it follows that the ratio of their marginal utilities to their marginal prices must be identical. If this were not so, obviously the system designer would spend the last dollar in enhancing the parameter for which this ratio is the highest because, then he or she would be able to enhance the utility to a higher value by using the same total amount of dollars.

Using this approach, one can determine which parameters best deserve to be improved from a user's standpoint when the overall utility is a known function of performance parameters.

8.4 OPTIMUM VALUE OF A PERFORMANCE PARAMETER

The previous section showed that the ratio of marginal utility of each performance parameter and the marginal cost of enhancing that parameter must be identical if resources are used optimally to enhance the utility of a system. Given the partial derivatives of the utility function and of the associated cost with respect to each of the performance parameters, one could evaluate whether the performance enhancement dollars have been distributed wisely among the different parameters.

Suppose, however, that the system designer was not resource-constrained. Suppose further that the system utility was related in a known way to, say, the profit associated with the system, which in turn is to be maximized. Under these assumptions, it is possible to determine the optimum performance level of each of the performance parameters. We illustrate this using the example of throughput as a performance parameter of a transmission system and assuming that it is proportional to, say, the revenue which in turn is to be maximized. The system cost is represented by the variable C. Assume that the initial conditions are as follows:

Initial Throughput = T_i

Total Initial System Cost = C_i

The starting throughput to cost ratio is therefore T_i / C_i. Now assume that an incremental enhancement δC to cost results in an incremental enhancement δT in the throughput, while the other performance parameters remain constant. It follows that the most desirable point to operate on the T-C continuum is one where T/C as a function C is a maximum, since this is the point where the output to input — or revenue to investment (or cost) — is the maximum. In order to meet the optimality condition, thus,

Optimum Value of a Performance Parameter

$$\frac{\delta(T/C)}{\delta C} = 0 \tag{8.5}$$

or,

$$\frac{\frac{\delta T}{\delta C} \cdot C - T}{C^2} = 0 \tag{8.6}$$

Equation (8.6) leads to the optimality condition,

$$T/C = \delta T/\delta C \tag{8.7}$$

implying that the marginal throughput to cost ratio ($\delta T/\delta C$) is equal to the average throughput to cost ratio.

Figure 8.1 shows a hypothetical situation. The peak of the T/C vs C curve corresponds to Equation (8.7). If the initial condition (T_i, C_i) were on the left-hand side of the peak, incurring additional cost would be justified to improve the performance parameter under consideration. However, if the initial condition were on the right-hand side of the peak, incurring additional cost would not be justified. Since it is entirely possible that any change in an

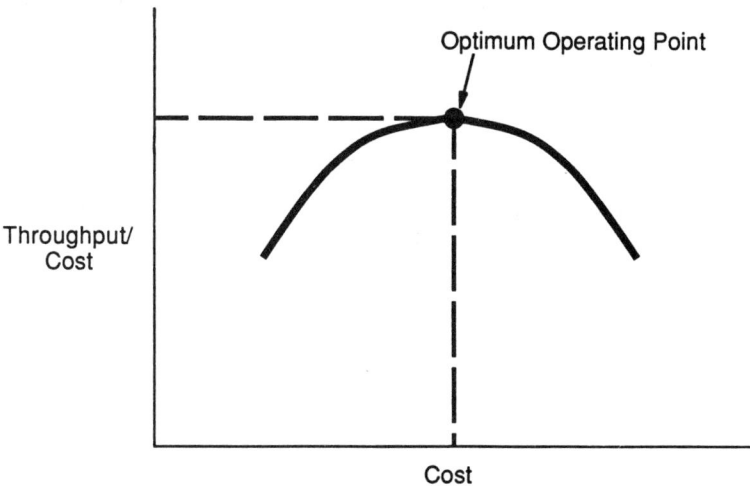

Figure 8.1
Determination of Optimum Performance Parameters

existing system will result in additional net cost, in situations where the initial condition is on the right-hand side of the peak, it will not be desirable to incur additional cost to enhance performance.

Unfortunately, in real situations, the parametric relationships are usually not known and an analytic approach as described above may be difficult to carry out. Reasonable approximations to the process described above may be carried out in these cases.

8.5 A NUMERICAL EXAMPLE

Consider the transmission system discussed in the last section and let its throughput T be considered as its utility or value. If the speed of the transmission system is s bits per second and its error rate p, then its throughput can be expressed as:

$$T = s(1 - p) \qquad (8.8)$$

The throughput can be improved by reducing the error rate p which in turn will require additional costs to be incurred. The error rate p is a function of the repeater spacing d (miles) and can be expressed as, say,*

$$p = ad \qquad (8.9)$$

where a is a constant.

Let the total cost C of the transmission system be expressed as the sum of a fixed cost C_1 and a variable cost which is inversely proportional to the repeater spacings d, that is,

$$C = C_1 + C_2/d \qquad (8.10)$$

where C_1 and C_2 are constants.

The problem is to determine the optimum value of the performance parameter p.

We have, from Section 8.4, the condition of optimality as:

$$\frac{T}{C} = \frac{\delta T}{\delta C} \qquad (8.11)$$

---

* In actual practice, the error rate is a much more complex function of the repeater spacing.

Using Equations (8.8) and (8.10), we have

$$\frac{T}{C} = \frac{s(1-p)}{C_1 + C_2/d} \qquad (8.12)$$

Using Equation (8.9) in Equation (8.12), we get

$$\frac{T}{C} = \frac{s(1-ad)}{C_1 + C_2/d} \qquad (8.13)$$

From Equation (8.8) we can write

$$\frac{\delta T}{\delta C} = \frac{\delta s(1-p)}{\delta C}$$

$$= \frac{s \cdot \delta(1-ad)}{\delta C} \quad \text{using Equation (8.9)}$$

$$= s \cdot \frac{\delta}{\delta C}\left[1 - \frac{aC_2}{C - C_1}\right] \quad \text{using Equation (8.10)}$$

$$= -asC_2 \frac{\delta}{\delta C} \frac{1}{C - C_1}$$

$$= \frac{asC_2}{(C - C_1)^2} \qquad (8.14)$$

From Equations (8.13) and (8.14), we can now write the optimality condition as,

$$\frac{s(1-ad)}{C_1 + C_2/d} = \frac{asC_2}{(C - C_1)^2}$$

or

$$\frac{1-ad}{C_1 + C_2/d} = \frac{ad^2}{C_2} \quad \text{using Equation (8.10)} \qquad (8.15)$$

After some algebraic simplification, Equation (8.15) can be written as:

$$aC_1 d^2 + 2aC_2 d - C_2 = 0$$

or

$$d = \frac{-2aC_2 \pm \sqrt{4a^2 C_2^2 + 4aC_1 C_2}}{2aC_1} \qquad (8.16)$$

Knowing that d can only be positive, we can rewrite Equation (8.16) as:

$$d = \frac{-aC_2 + \sqrt{a^2 C_2^2 + aC_1 C_2}}{aC_1} \qquad (8.17)$$

For example, if

$$a = 10^{-5} \text{ (miles}^{-1})$$

$$C_1 = 100{,}000 \text{ (\$)}$$

$$C_2 = 10 \text{(\$ mile)}$$

we have

$$d = 3.162 \text{ miles}$$

The variation of the throughput to cost ratio as a function of repeater spacing is diagrammed in Figure 8.2.

From the numerical results obtained above, the optimum value of the performance parameter p can be derived using Equation (8.9) as:

$$p = ad$$

$$= 3.162 \times 10^{-5}$$

A Numerical Example

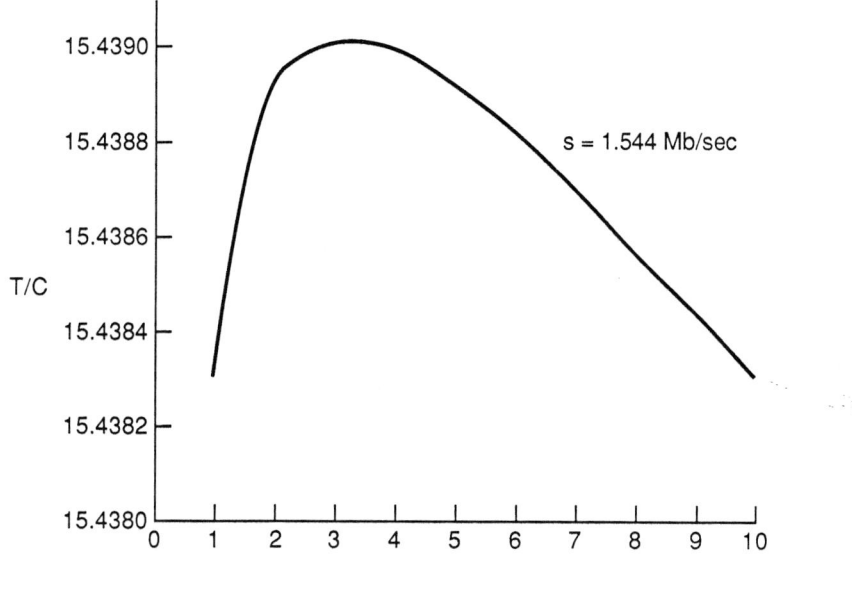

Figure 8.2
Optimal Repeater Spacing

APPENDIX

NETWORK SWITCHING TECHNIQUES AND THEIR CHARACTERISTICS

This appendix provides a general introduction to the switching techniques used in communication networks. A qualitative discussion of the different switching techniques is made in order to provide an insight into their applicability to computer traffic of different characteristics.

A.1 AN OVERVIEW OF A NETWORK

A network is physically realized as a collection of nodes and interconnecting transmission channels. Nodes are responsible for processing and storage as well as switching. In conjunction with the interconnecting transmission channels, the nodal switching system provides an internodal transport structure for conveying information from one node to another. Figure A.1 shows a computer communication network. The transport structure is comprised of the transmission facilities and part of the node involved in carrying out the internodal switching function, shown hatched in Figure A.1. The internodal transport structure can use a variety of switching options depending upon the traffic characteristics and performance requirements. In this appendix we examine the characteristics of different switching techniques.

A.2 TYPES OF SWITCHING

Two or more end points are said to be connected by a private line if they can communicate at a constant transmission speed all the time. A network of private lines without any switching facility constitutes a transmission network. As mentioned in Chapter 1, AT&T's DDS system is a transmission network

Types of Switching

[1]. A private line connecting two end points provides a point-to-point transmission facility. If a multiplicity of end points share the same private line transmission facility, they are said to be communicating on a multipoint basis. Multipoint facilities are shared by more than two end points by using a contention or a polling mechanism to allocate the transmission resource to the

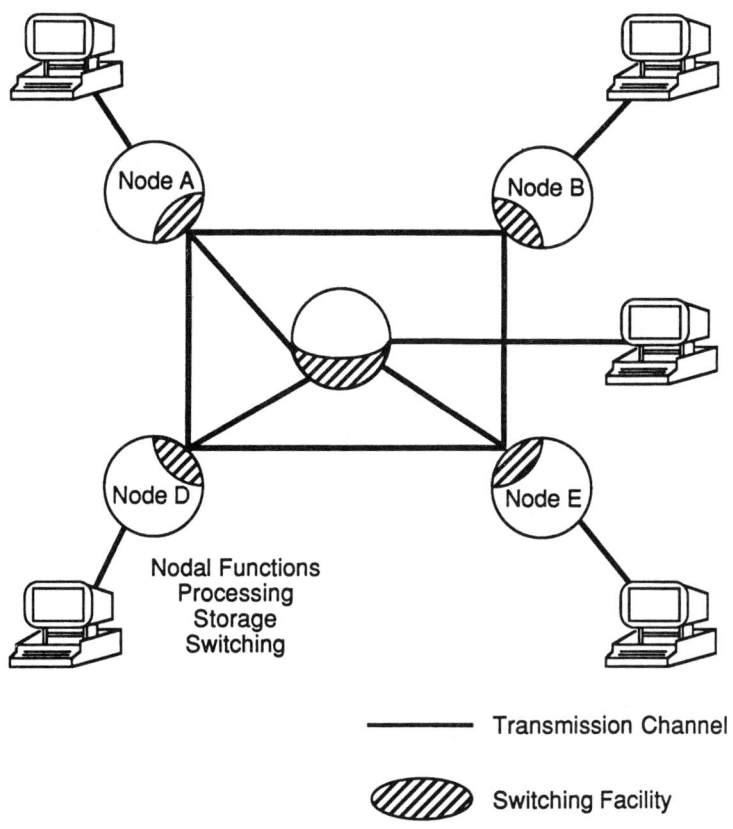

Figure A.1
A Computer Communication Network

appropriate pair of end points desiring communication. Usually, this appropriate pair includes one master station, the communication being directed between the master station and one of the others. A broadcast option includes the master station transmitting information to all the other stations simultaneously. The private line point-to-point and multipoint systems are shown in Figures A.2 and A.3 respectively.

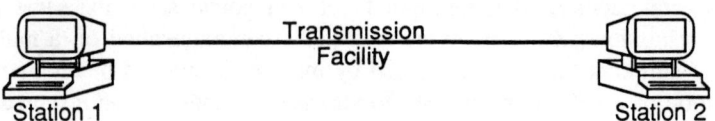

Figure A.2
Private Line Point-to-Point System

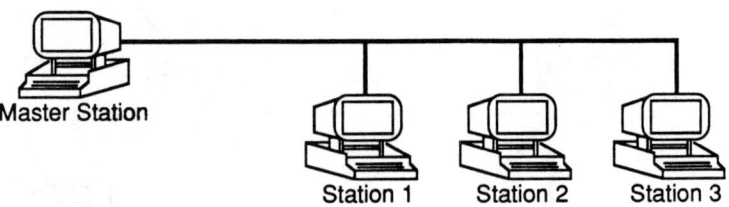

Figure A.3
Private Line Multipoint System

The primary motivation for a multipoint system is realizing savings in transmission costs. Multipoint networking, in general, suffers from a number of performance problems. Nevertheless, it has been popular in computer networking because of its cost savings in comparison to leasing a number of point-to-point transmission facilities.

Figure A.4 shows part of a transport tree depicting the switched and private line options.

A switched transport network is one where any two (or more) end points could communicate on demand. The public switched network is an example of a switched network which can provide a connection on demand between any two telephones. For most applications, where a permanent association between end points is not needed, a switched network provides a highly cost-effective solution.

There are two basic types of switching: circuit switching and store and forward switching. In circuit switching, a physical, real time, and constant bandwidth or bit rate channel is provided between the communicating end points for the entire duration of connection. For example, in the public switched network, a channel of 4-kHz nominal bandwidth is set up between the calling and the called parties for the entire duration of the time for which the call is up. A succession of switching machines may have to be involved in the setting up of a single call. Each machine will reserve a physical association between one incoming and one outgoing channel at 4 kHz or 64

Kb/sec. Unless the entire end-to-end channel has been set up, the transfer of information cannot be initiated in circuit switching.

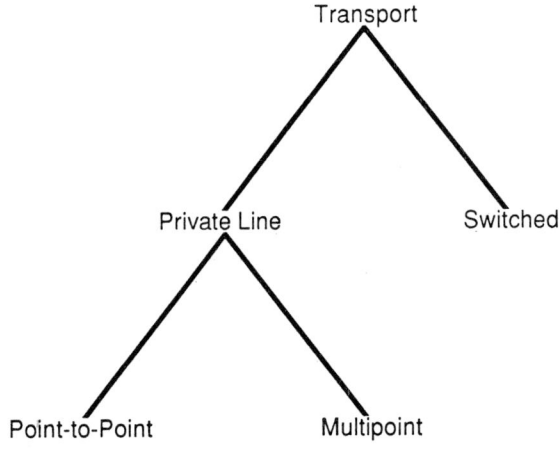

Figure A.4
The Transport Tree

Store and forward switching, on the other hand, uses a technique whereby an end-to-end transmission channel between the source and the destination does not have to be set up before the calling entity can deliver information to the network. The calling entity communicates only with the nearest node of the network and hands over to it the information bits, which are stored by the accepting node, and then forwarded through a succession of nodes, as necessary, to the ultimate destination. Each node in store and forward switching has to be equipped with a sufficient amount of storage, depending upon the volume of traffic it anticipates. The two primary options in switched transport are illustrated in Figure A.5.

In circuit switching, if the called party is busy or if at least one of the switching machines in the chain required to set up the call could not do so, then the call is blocked and the originating customer, usually, must try again at a later time. The store and forward switching has no blocking associated with it, since a real-time connectivity between the calling and the called end points is not desired. The storage at each node, in store and forward switching, can be made large enough to ensure that customer data can be accepted with a very high probability. The postal system can be characterized as an example of store and forward switching. Here, the chance that the mail box is too full to accept a letter is extremely small. When the postal volume exceeds the capacity of the system temporarily, delay in the delivery of the mail results. 'Blocking' and 'delay' can thus be seen to be corresponding attributes of circuit and store and forward switching, respectively.

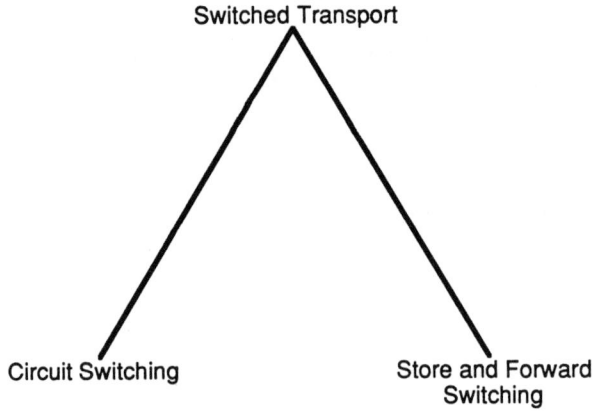

Figure A.5
Options in Switched Transport

One can also make the following inferences about the two basic switching techniques. Irrespective of the number of nodes or switching machines between the source and the destination, circuit switching provides both bit sequence transparency and time transparency as defined in Section 3.2. Bit sequence transparency is a necessary requirement for all store and forward networks. Time transparency, in general, is not guaranteed by store and forward networks.

The initial time needed to set up the end-to-end channel in circuit switching is usually large since, in general, the cooperation of a number of switching machines is essential in this process. Once the connection has been set up, the switching nodes are performing a minimal amount of function, however, and a large volume of information could be transferred without incurring any additional overhead in setting up the channel. It can be concluded that there are two components of resource consumption in transporting information using the circuit switching technique:

- Resources to set up the call

- Resources to keep up the switching machine cross points or the time slot mappings and the transmission links

The first category of resource consumption, that is, the resource required to set up the call, is independent of the volume of information transmitted. The second component is directly proportional to the duration of time for which the call is up. The cost of transferring information using the circuit switching technique can thus be idealized as shown in Figure A.6. The cost of setting up the call is represented by a point P; the slope of the (linear) cost curve represents the cost of switching, through a number of machines and the use of transmission facilities, as a function of time. The linear nature of the curve is explained by the volume being directly proportional to time since the bit rate is constant and predefined in circuit switched communication. It can be readily concluded that if any of the switching machines in the chosen path to the destination is fully occupied, or if any of the links in the path is busy, or if the destination is busy, the end-to-end channel can't be set up.

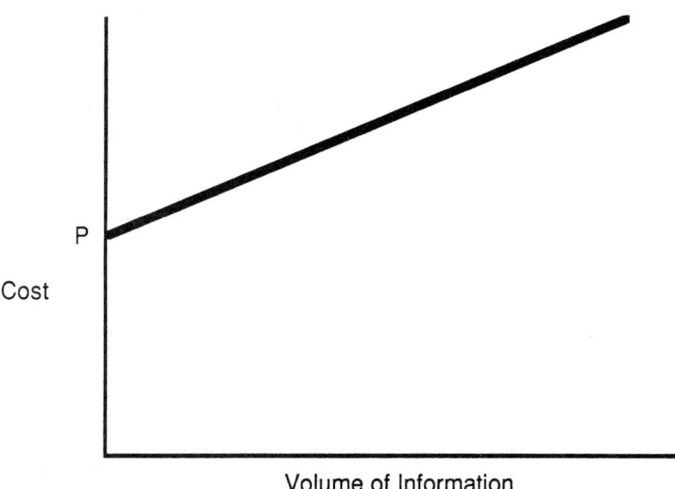

Figure A.6
Cost Characteristics of a Circuit Switched Network

In store and forward switching, the information to be transmitted will be stored at each node on way to the destination. The delay due to storage will in general be different at each node.

Use of a storage medium provides considerable flexibility. It implies that the switching and transmission resources between the calling and the called ends do not all have to be ready at the same time. With sufficient storage at each node, the store and forward switching will result in the user seldom encountering a blocking situation as discussed earlier. The practical implementation of the store and forward switching technique is in one of the following forms:

- Message switching
- Packet switching
- Character switching

These are discussed in the following sections.

A.3 MESSAGE SWITCHING

In message switching, the entire message retains its integrity as a single entity during its passage from one node to another. Since a message has no defined length, it will vary widely between small and large messages. The requirement to retain the single message as a whole during its passage through the network results in rather severe requirements on buffer sizes to take care of the occasional large messages. In addition, a transit node cannot start passing on part of a message it is still receiving. This results in (avoidable) delays as well as potentially poor utilization of network resources.

Even though several message switching systems have been built and many of them are still operating, message switching is increasingly giving way to packet switching, particularly in common user environments.

A.4 PACKET SWITCHING

In packet switching, a message is broken into smaller units, each with its own address and possibly different routing information. A packet is usually a few hundred characters long, with all characters in the packet belonging to the same user. Packets are transported on a store and forward basis across the intermediate nodes.

Packet switching allows pipelining of the network resources since larger messages are broken down into smaller units and can be acted upon independently by different nodes simultaneously. Overall, this results in reduction of delay, enhancement of network throughput and better utilization of network resources. Compared to circuit switching, packet switching entails considerably additional processing resources. In an attempt to idealize the cost characteristics of a packet switched network, consider the following: The two components of resource consumption in a packet switched network operating on a virtual circuit principle [2] are:

- Resources to set up the virtual channel
- Resources to process each packet of information

The resource to set up a virtual channel should be considerably smaller than the resource required to set up a physical channel on an end-to-end basis. Further, the network resource required to process packets through the network is directly proportional to the number of packets. For a message which is several packets long, the switching cost is thus directly proportional to the length of the message.

One characteristic of all store and forward switching techniques is to permit speed matching between the source and the destination. This capability exists because the source and the destination are effectively decoupled by storage within the network. Packet switched networks can thus be used to transfer the same volume of information at a variety of speeds within a specified range of access speeds. The network switching cost will be, to a first approximation, identical in each case. The access speed can be chosen to match the delay performance requirements. The higher the access speed, the lower the delay perceived by the user. Of course, higher access speeds are associated with correspondingly higher access costs.

If we attempt to plot the cost characteristics of packet switching as a function of volume of information on a scale identical to that in Figure A.6, the intersection of the packet switching cost characteristics with the cost axis will be lower than the corresponding point for the circuit switched case. However, the slope of the packet switching cost characteristics will be higher, since subsequent to setting up of the virtual circuit, considerably more processing effort is warranted in transferring information in a store and forward mode. A comparison of the circuit and packet switching cost characteristics as a function of the volume of information transferred is illustrated in Figure A.7. The intersection point Q of the two curves

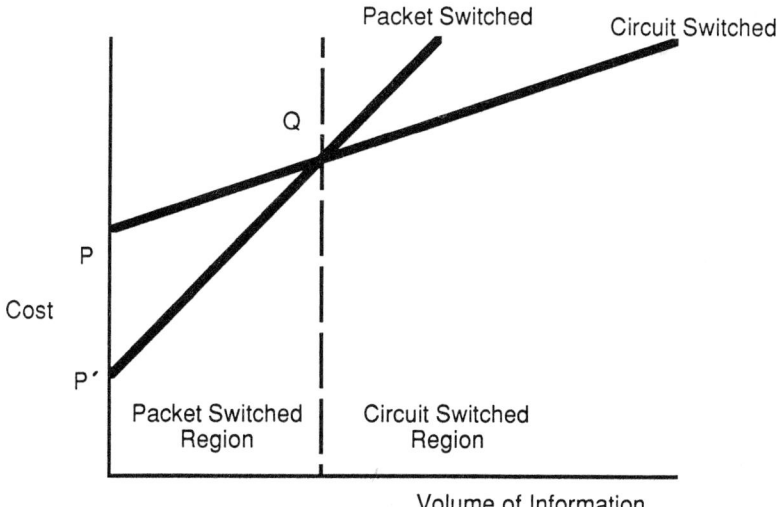

Figure A.7
A Comparison of Switching Costs

delineates the two areas in which circuit and packet switching are cost effective.

For the sake of completeness, one can superimpose on Figure A.7 the cost characteristics of a private line between the two end points. A private line circuit has a high initial cost but no switching costs associated with it. The inclusion of a private line in Figure A.7 results in Figure A.8. Figure A.8 illustrates the regions of applicability of the different switching techniques as a function of the volume of information to be transferred. Information volumes greater than the abscissa of point Q' are cost effectively addressed by a private line solution. In delineating the cost effective regions in Figure A.8, it should be remembered that the comparisons are valid only as long as performance requirements are met by each of the alternatives considered.

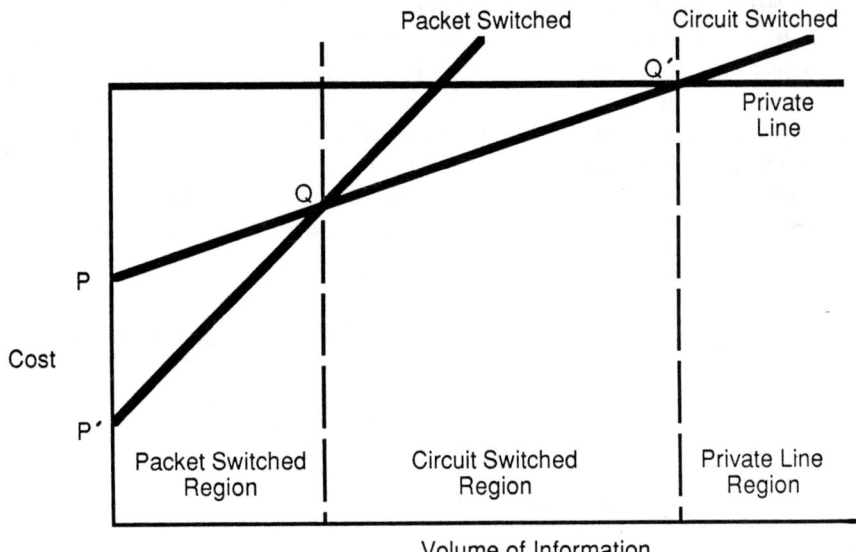

Figure A.8
Cost Characteristics of Circuit and Packet
Switching and Private Line

A.4.1 Further Characteristics of Packet Switching

We have seen in the last section that, under certain assumptions, the network cost of transferring information using packet switching technology is directly proportional to the volume of information, and is independent of the speed of access. Using this fact we can derive some interesting conclusions.

Let us assume we wish to describe a particular transaction involving transfer of data between two end points on a speed-holding time plane. For a given volume v of data transfer, the access speed s and holding time t are related by the following equation:

$$v = st \qquad (A.1)$$

On the speed-holding time (s-t) plane, this transaction is described as, say, a point P. A constant volume curve on this plane is a rectangular hyperbola described by Equation (A.1). The volume v is therefore constant anywhere on the curve described by Equation (A.1), while s and t may assume different pairs of values (see Figure A.9).

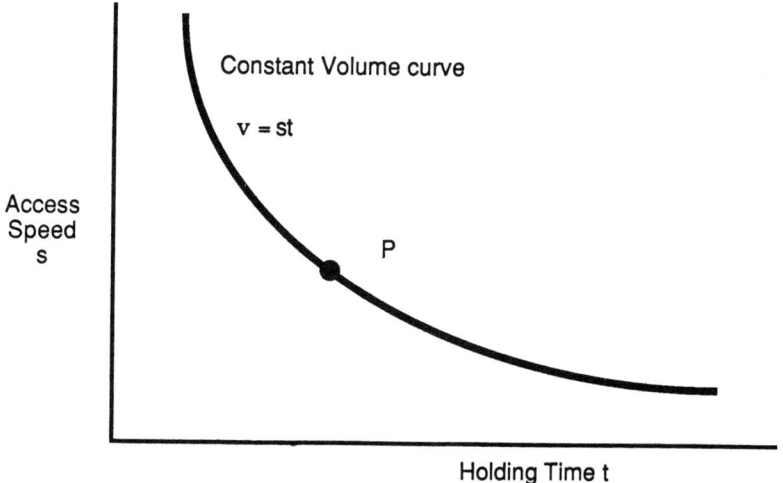

Figure A.9
Speed-Holding Time Characteristics of Packet Switching

Anywhere on this curve, the network switching cost will be identical; while the access cost will be higher, as the access speed s increases. The user will generally choose to operate at the lowest access speed consistent with the delay performance requirements being met.

If the curve shown in Figure A.9 represented the volume corresponding to point Q of Figure A.7, then every point below the curve would be best served by packet switching, while every point on the other side of the curve would be best served by circuit switching. One must remember, however, that a circuit switched network does not have the same choice of speed options as a packet switched network. If, in circuit switching, a single speed option* s_1 is available then all points on the right-hand side of (or above) the curve will have to be mapped on a straight line with equation

$$s = s_1 \qquad (A.2)$$

A particular point with coordinates t_2, s_2 in the circuit switched region will be transferred to the straight line described by Equation (A.2) with its t-coordinate given by

$$t = \frac{t_2 s_2}{s_1} \qquad (A.3)$$

This is shown in Figure A.10.

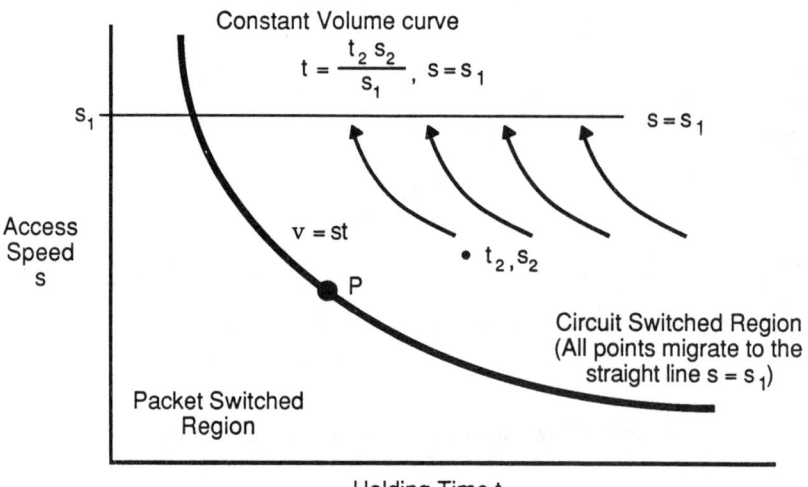

Figure A.10
Packet and Circuit Switching Traffic Segmentation

---

* For example, the Integrated Services Digital Network (ISDN) recommends a speed of 64 kilobits per second for communication among end points.

A.5 CHARACTER SWITCHING

As discussed in Section A.4 of this Appendix, the fundamental motivation for packet switching arose from the need to obtain a better delay performance in a store and forward environment. In packet switching systems, the packet is an independent entity with the ability to direct itself to the destination node according to the routing discipline adopted by the network. A variation of the packet switching technique, called character switching, results when a packet contains information bits belonging to more than one user. This technique is also referred to as the public packet approach.

The choice of the maximum permissible packet size in a packet switched network is governed by three basic considerations: (a) distribution of message lengths, (b) transmission environment, and (c) overhead considerations. The conflicting requirements of lower delays and efficient transmission are usually met through a compromise.

Admission delay is a component of the overall or end-to-end delay in any packet switched network. It is defined as the delay incurred on the periphery of the network before packetization and subsequent transfer of information begins. This component becomes a predominant component when the access line speeds are low. For example, a 1000-bit message transferred within a 1000-bit packet will incur an admission delay of 3.3 seconds if a 300-baud access line is chosen. (See Chapter 3.) One alternative to lowering the admission delay is to lower the packet sizes. However, this may be uneconomic if the packet overhead becomes unacceptably large as a result.

The public packet approach retains the optimum packet size as applicable to the transmission environment while at the same time reducing the admission delay. The latter is accomplished by choosing a smaller number of characters from several subscribers and transporting them in a "public" packet. Using the former example, if a public packet is used for carrying messages from three subscribers instead of a single one, the admission delay will be reduced to 1.1 sec from 3.3 sec.

It may appear at first sight that additional overhead bits will inevitably be needed in the public packets in order to retain the identity of the several pieces of information belonging to different users. A suitable choice of architecture may alleviate this problem in order to make the overall scheme more attractive compared to conventional packet switching for the class of low-speed asynchronous unbuffered terminals where the access delays are substantial.

For example, the Tymnet network [3,4] substantially reduces the overheads required by maintaining a fixed shortest-path, least-cost routing throughout the entire duration of a session or call. Messages arriving at a node are stored in character buffers and each message has a channel number associated with it. Message transmission to the adjacent node is effected by assembling a public packet for each outgoing link. The assembly is done by searching through the buffers for characters belonging to messages with channel numbers associated with the link on which the packet is to be transmitted. The packet format consists of a header (with synchronization pattern, size number and acknowledgments), user messages (each with a channel number and length), and error detection characters. The total maximum packet size is 66 characters.

Character switching can be considered as subpacket switching. Character switching entails a low initial call-set-up cost, but the costs associated with information transfer subsequent to the call-set-up rise faster than those of packet switching as a function of volume of information. This latter phenomenon is attributable to the fact that additional subpacket-level processing requirements also exist in character switching. Figure A.8 can be augmented to include character switching cost characteristics. This is illustrated in Figure A.11.

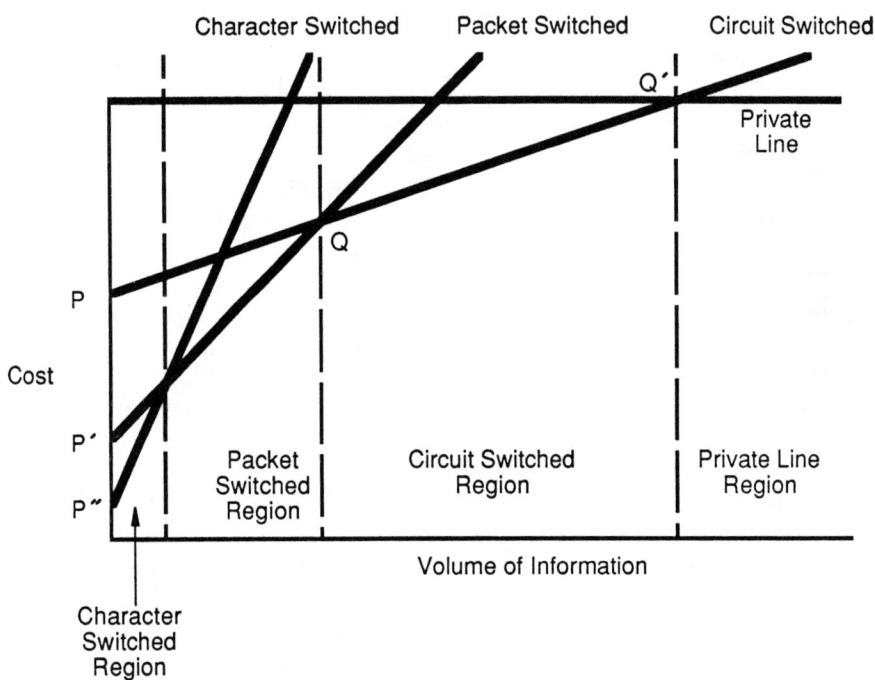

Figure A.11
Cost Characteristics of Circuit, Packet, and Character Switching, and Private Line

Message switching, packet switching and character switching are the primary variants of store and forward switching (see Figure A.12). Of course,

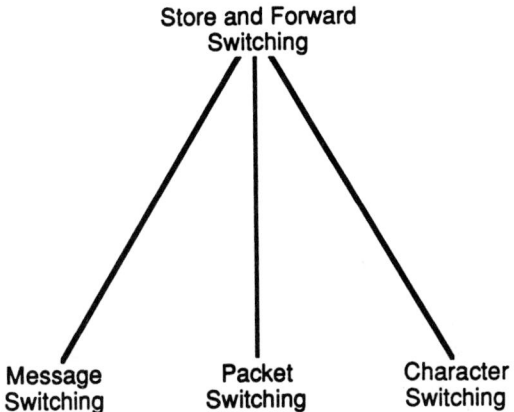

Figure A.12
Primary Variants of Store and Forward Switching

Table A.1
Major Characteristics of Switching Technologies

	Private Line	*Circuit*	*Packet*	*Character*
Blocking	No	Yes	No	No
Utilization of Transmission Facilities	Fully Dedicated	Dedicated To a Single User While Call Is Up	Not Dedicated	Not Dedicated
Call Set-Up Delay	None	High	Low	Low
Speed Matching Capability	No	No	Yes	Yes
Transparency In Time	Yes	Yes	No	No
Bit Sequence Transparency	Yes	Yes	Yes	Yes

combinations of these three techniques can result in additional switching techniques to handle heterogeneous traffic more effectively than a single technique. The major characteristics of the switching techniques are reviewed in Table A.1.

A.6 REFERENCES

[1] N. E. Snow and N. Knapp, Jr., "Digital Data System: System Overview," <u>The Bell System Technical Journal</u>, Vol. 54, No. 5, May-June 1975, pp. 811-832.

[2] J. R. Hasley, L. E. Hardy, and L. F. Powning, "Public Data Networks: Their Evolution, Interfaces and Status," <u>IBM Systems Journal</u>, Vol. 18, No. 2, 1979, pp. 223-244.

[3] L. R. Tymes, "Tymnet—A Terminal Oriented Communication Network," <u>AFIPS Conf. Proc.</u>, Vol. 38, 1971, pp. 211-216.

[4] M. Schwartz, R. R. Boorstyn, and R. L. Pichholtz, "Terminal Oriented Computer Communication Networks," <u>Proc. IEEE</u>, Vol. 60, No. 11, November 1972, pp. 1408-1423.

INDEX

Admission delay, 127
Assembly delay, 83
Asynchronous transmission, 30
Average assembly delay, 93-96

Baud, 6, 29, 30, 32, 127
Bit error rate, 44, 45, 54
Bits per second, 30
Block error rate, 45, 52, 54, 55, 66
Block oriented terminal, 74, 75, 82-84, 86, 87, 95

Character-at-a-time terminal, 74, 75 78, 82, 84-87, 95
Character error rate, 44
Character switching, 127, 128
Circuit switching, 118-128
Coding,
  duobinary, 23
  extension of duobinary, 25
  partial response, 23
Computer communication, 11, 41
  history of development in, 1, 5
  network model, 11, 41, 42
Computer communication networks,
  architecture, 4
  elements, 3
  resources, 4
Cost,
  additions, reduction,
    and rearrangement, 16
  displaced, 17
  exit, 16
  fixed recurring, 16
  start-up, 16
  usage-sensitive, 16

Cyclic coding, 62, 63
Cyclic redundancy coding, 62, 67, 71, 72

Data, 2
Data transmission network, 6
Data transmission system, 31
Dataroute, 6, 9, 26, 58
Delay(s),
  components, 80
  elements of end-to-end, 78
  end-to-end, 74-79, 82, 87, 88, 97, 127
  propagation, 66
Digital data system, 69, 130

End point, 2, 6-8, 15, 28, 42, 116-119, 124-126
End-to-end delay, 74, 75, 78, 79 82, 87, 88, 97, 127
Error correction,
  backward, 59, 60, 62
  forward, 59, 60, 62
  techniques for, 59
Error environment, 59
Error-free seconds, 54

Information and communication, 2
Information society,
  transition to, 1, 3
Interference delay, 79, 80, 82
International Standards
  Organization, 41, 72

Layered model, 41

Mean error-free interval, 46
Message assembly protocols, 75
Modem, 5, 19, 20, 75

Network architecture, 4
Nodes, 3
Noise,
  penalty of, 21
Nonoperational state, 39-41
Nyquist's principle, 20, 22

Operational state, 39, 40

Packet switched networks, 74-78, 82,
    83, 85-88, 95, 97, 102, 103, 105,
    122, 123, 126, 127
  end-to-end delays in, 74, 75, 78, 79,
    82, 87, 88, 97, 127
Performance objectives, 107
Performance parameters,
  accuracy, 14
  availability, 14
  categories of, 13
  delay, 13
  throughput, 13

Price,
  pricing structure, 15
Public packet, 127

Response time(s),
  mean, 75, 85, 86, 95
  percentile, 95

Signal-to-noise ratio, 18, 19
Synchronous transmission, 30
  system, 31

Throughput, 13
Transit delay, 79
Transmission,
  accuracy of, 32
  integrity of, 32
  synchronous and
    asynchronous, 18, 29, 30
Transmission medium,
  capacity, 18
  characteristics of, 18, 27
  delay in, 29
  noise, 20
Transmission-level performance, 43
Tymnet network, 75, 77, 127, 130

ABOUT THE AUTHOR

Pramode K. Verma is with AT&T Bell Laboratories in Lincroft, New Jersey, and currently manages a group engaged in multivendor networking and connectivity verification. He joined AT&T in 1978, and has moved through a variety of positions at Bell Laboratories: General Departments, Product Management, and Marketing, prior to assuming his current position in 1984. One of his areas of activity has been performance assessment of computer communication networks and systems.

During 1971-78, he was a Supervising Engineer with the Computer Communications Group of Bell Canada, Ottawa, and worked on the design of Canada's nationwide networks, the Dataroute and Datapac. Prior to that, he worked as an Assistant Professor in the Faculty of Engineering at Concordia University. He has also served as an Adjunct Assistant Professor at the University of Ottawa (1974-77), and as an Adjunct Professor at Concordia University (1984-86). He worked with the Indian Posts and Telegraphs Department, New Delhi, India, during 1964-67, and the Indian Institute of Science, Bangalore, India, during 1962-64.

Dr. Verma obtained his doctorate in Electrical Engineering from Concordia University in 1970, a Bachelor's degree in Engineering in 1962 from the Indian Institute of Science, Bangalore, and a Bachelor's degree in Science (Honors) in 1959 from the Patna University, Patna. In 1984, he also obtained an M.B.A. from the Wharton School of the University of Pennsylvania. He is the author of over thirty publications in telecommunications, computer communications and related fields. His other professional accomplishments include: Program Chairman and Editor of the Proceedings of the Third International Conference on Computer Communication, Toronto, 1976; Conference Governor of the Eighth Conference on Computer Communication, Munich, 1986; Editor, Journal of Telecommunication Networks, 1982-85; and Contributor to the McGraw Hill Encyclopedia of Science and Technology (Sixth Edition). He is listed in the American Men and Women of Science, published by Jacques Cattel Press.

SOUTHEASTERN MASSACHUSETTS UNIVERSITY
TK5105.5.V47 1989
Performance estimation of computer commu

3 2922 00046 696 8

WITHDRAWN